MW01265042

The Idiocy of Perfection

Jesús Silva-Herzog Márquez

English translation by Tanya Huntington

literalpublishing

First edition, 2017

5425 Renwick Dr.
Houston , TX 77081
www.literalmagazine.com

ISBN: 978-1-942307-13-6

Printed & Bounced by The Country Press, Inc. P. O. Box 489
Middleborough, MA 02346-0489

Not for us such idiotic
onionoid perfections.

Wisława Szymborska

Table Of Contents

Introduction

What I offer here is a handful of portraits: essays about five men who rethought politics in the final stretch of the 20th century. By which I do not mean to imply that they were zeniths of their time. If my criteria were orographic, this would be quite a different gallery. These figures are not linked by any common cause, temperament, or misfortune. In terms of selection, it isn't academic rigor that reveals itself in these sketches, but rather one reader's caprice. A jurist, a biographer, a professor, a historian, and a poet: Carl Schmitt, Isaiah Berlin, Norberto Bobbio, Michael Oakeshott, and Octavio Paz. None of whom, just to be clear from the start, fits neatly into the box of a square filing cabinet: a desperate socialist, an adventurous conservative, a lawyer who upheld unlawfulness, a lonely man nostalgic for fraternity, a conflicted liberal.

Although no common thread joins their ideas or talents, a bridge could perhaps be found spanning the expanse of their quandaries. As they oscillated between definition and metaphor, in poems and speeches along the corridors of memory or imagination (which, according to Hobbes, are one and the same), these authors sought to reach the core. They took on the major enigmas of politics, each in his own way. Are politics a sword that lends meaning to our existence, or simply a cruel form of entertainment? An efficient high command that moves the world, or a spectacle to mask our impotence? The heads or the tails of history? Conciliatory public square or battlefield? Civilizing hope, or untamable beast?

What I mean to say is that these men's intelligence did not merely scratch the surface. Digging beneath the skin of law and government, each of them carved out a spyhole through which he could examine the roots of politics: the nature of history and power; the *locus* of our reason, sense of smell, and inventiveness; the supremacy of rules and will; the shape of democracy; man's place among other men. For some, the hand of politics can do nothing more than take hold of a grenade and toss it at the enemy in hopes of destroying him. For others, politics is a ball with which we play while the clock keeps on ticking. An index finger that squeezes the trigger of a lethal weapon, or appeasingly extends a cup of coffee. Bombs or marbles: politics can either fire up the drama of war, or gradually take on the pointlessness of a game.

War or play, politics as outlined by these authors are one way of dealing with human imperfection. They see no sign of utopias, of paradises to be lost or gained. No shortcut to the end of times. Politics will always bear the fastidious marks of force, chance, and conflict: those stubborn naysayers of perfection.

Mexico City, July 29, 2005

The Science of Illegality

> Shall we dwell in catastrophe?
>
> Ernst Jünger

Carl Schmitt was born the same year as Adolf Hitler. Although they did coincide on one occasion, they never spoke to one another. The former felt a blend of disgust and fascination for the dictator; the latter never ascribed any importance whatsoever to the man who had offered to rationalize his abuses. This ambiguity would leave its mark on Carl Schmitt's entire life. And on his legacy as well. Parting from the emotional side of reason, he felt strongly repulsed by a man he considered to be crude, ignorant. He despised him as a rudimentary politician, incapable of articulating coherent discourse. Perhaps Schmitt also feared the violence that radiated from him. Yet his keen intuition also valued the strength and depth of his attraction. Hitler inexplicably embodied a mythic force: he was a man who, without calculation or debate, had perceived a chasm opening up underfoot. Hitler was power, energy. A blaze of enthusiasm and valor in the midst of lukewarm cowardice.

Just days before the electoral triumph of National Socialism, Carl Schmitt published an article in the press that foretold impending doom: whoever collaborated with the Nazis would be acting foolishly and irresponsibly. National Socialism, he argued, was a dangerous movement capable of altering the constitution, establishing a state church, dissolving labor unions, and crushing human rights. Less than a year later, by invitation of Heidegger, Carl Schmitt became a member of the National Socialist Party. Ambition, not his fear of the fledgling dictatorship, caused him to switch. Also, his conviction that the ugliness of power was always preferable to the horrors of anarchy. This is shown by an entry in his journal, dated the same day Hitler was named chancellor: "Irritated and somehow, relieved; *a decision, at least.*" Through Hitler, hope for determination surged. Carl Schmitt met Hitler on April 7, 1933. The Führer was scheduled to present his political agenda. The encounter was recorded in one of Schmitt's private journals. The room was crammed with steely-eyed party and military hierarchs, all of whom watched their Leader closely. Hitler acted like a bull nervously entering the ring. Thirty minutes went by, and the speech still hadn't come anywhere close to taking off. Hitler is portrayed in Schmitt's notes as insecure, hanging obsessively on the reactions of his audience. Like a patient on life support, this speaker needed the artificial respirator of applause. Everyone listened closely, and... nothing. From up close, the great agitator of the masses turned out to be an insipid little orator. The Führer made no real connection with his audience, communicated no memorable ideas, fired no lightning bolts. Nothing.

The lawyer's disappointment remained hidden behind his opportunistic calculations. One had to join the winning side, after all. Four weeks after this encounter, he was assigned Party credential number 2,098,860. And the mask of devotion worked, at least for the time being. Soon, he would become a valuable cog in the machinery of nationalist legitimization: legal apostle to the new regime. The official newspaper of Nazism dubbed him the "crown jurist," an investiture that was by no means undeserved –at least during the early stage of Nazism, when he in essence acted as the legal mind behind German fascism. Schmitt saw the new order as an opportunity to launch a great legal revolution, one that would abandon the arguments of a "decrepit era." His objective was to revive the law, reconciling it with justice through the savior-like intervention of a strongman. Given that the old legal framework had decayed under the rule of law, the new one would have to rediscover morality (even if it meant crushing said rule of law). Thus, a coup d'etat could become "rigorously legal." A violation of statutes could become a defense of the basic rights of the German people. It was the birth of a new legality.

Schmitt intended to outline a legal philosophy that would break away from the liberal, bourgeois model. One of the key principles of legality would have to be demolished. Here, he was referring to that fundamental maxim of criminal law, which establishes that there can be no punishment other than those already established.

> Everyone understands that it is a requirement of justice to punish crimes. Those who [...] constantly spoke of the "*Rechtsstaat*" did not place primary importance on the fact that an evil crime found a just punishment. For them the issue lay in a different principle, which, according to the situation, can lead to the op-

> posite of a just punishment, namely the *Rechtsstaat* principle: no punishment without a law, *nulla poena sine lege*. [By contrast, those] who think justly in a case see to it that no crime remains without a punishment. I pit this *Rechtsstaat* principle *nulla poena sine lege* against the principle of justice, "*nulla crimen sine poena*" (no crime without a punishment). The discrepancy between the *Rechtsstaat* and the Just State then becomes immediately visible.[1]

The Penal Code, Schmitt grumbled, had become a Magna Carta for criminals. Rules shouldn't pose an obstacle to punishment. A weak age had handed down these cowardly principles, thus sanctifying procedure and sheltering crime. That is why it had become vital to substitute these malleable statutes with the virility of forceful power.

The man who had once denounced the dark dangers of Nazism went above and beyond the call of duty in defending the new regime. He praised the purges that wound up executing dissidents as if they were beautiful formulas of revolutionary justice, and espoused the purification of German judicial theory. He wasn't weighing methodological reform, but rather the need to eliminate Jewish contamination. Books written by Jews were to be removed from the libraries; and if anyone attempted to refer to the ideas of a Jewish writer, he should indicate, as if on a health warning label, that this notion had come out of the enemy camp. Hans Kelsen, the great jurist of the century, suffered the brunt of the commissar's attacks. He had supported Schmitt when he joined the University

---

[1] Cited in Balakrishnan, *The Enemy. An Intellectual Portrait of Carl Schmitt* (London: Verso, 2000), p. 12.

of Cologne, despite the differences separating them and Schmitt's harsh critiques of his work. Some time later, the founder of the Pure Theory of Law was struck down by the Nazi purges: while vacationing in Sweden, Kelsen was expelled from the university. The professors of the Faculty of Law met immediately to request the reinstatement of the staff's most prestigious professor. The only academic who refused to sign the petition was Carl Schmitt. His attitude regarding the purge was not one of simple indifference before the defenestration of his former supporter. He actively took part in having him thrown out onto the street. As the secretary of his great friend, Ernst Jünger, had already noted: "Try not to cross Schmitt! You could end up in a concentration camp!"[2]

CARL SCHMITT WAS BORN ON JULY 11, 1888, TO A HUMBLE household in Plettenberg, a small town ensconced in central Germany. Johann, his father, was a loyal member of the Catholic party who worked at the train station and supported the local church. At home, Carl's mother cultivated a certain nostalgia for her French roots. French airs and hard-boiled Catholicism marked him as a child. From a very early age, his bonds to the Latin world would press upon him a gentle awareness of his foreignness. "I am Roman by origin, tradition and right," he would sententiously claim on one occasion.

The doors of the world swung open before his intelligence. He left the hamlet of Plettenberg in order to study

[2] The expression is Hugo Fisher's and is referred to by Jean-Pierre Faye in *Los lenguajes totalitarios* (Madrid: Taurus, 1974), p. 112. Translator's note: henceforth, unless otherwise noted, this and all other English translations of quotes are mine.

first at the Attendorn preparatory school, then at the University of Berlin. It was there in Attendorn that he took his first steps toward an education in the humanities. It was also where his love for languages flourished: Latin, Greek, Spanish and Italian. In 1907, he arrived in Berlin to start his professional studies. He had leaned toward philology but in the end, opted for law: an uncle had convinced him it was the more profitable profession.

His encounter with this formidable university and imposing city was disconcerting. As Joseph Roth would write years later, Berlin was its own capital. A city populated by the world's most ghastly churches; a city that had "no society," but nonetheless offered all that was necessary: people, theaters, museums, art, bars, shops.[3] To the young student, the city must have seemed a terrible, fascinating spectacle, machinery that turned men into ants. Schmitt, like Roth, would feel the crush of the city as an ominous technological empire.

Perhaps he never freed himself of the sensation of being a foreigner in the heart of his own country. This was a feeling that had originated long ago and would stay with him always.

> I was an obscure young man of modest descent... Neither the ruling strata nor the opposition included me... That meant that I, standing entirely in the dark, out of the darkness looked into a brightly lit room... The feeling of sadness which filled me made me more distant and awoke in others mistrust and antipathy. The ruling strata experienced

[3] See Joseph Roth, *What I Saw. Reports from Berlin 1920-1933* (New York and London: W.W. Norton & Company, 2002).

> anybody who was not thrilled to be involved with them as heterogeneous. It put before him the choice to adapt or to withdraw. So I remained outside.[4]

Schmitt, a Catholic in a land of Evangelists, a Latin among Prussians, felt like an outsider. He was a short man, not 5'3" tall. Shy, quiet, a loner. "My nature," he wrote as an old man, "is slow, silent and easy-going, like a still river, like the Moselle."[5] He contemplated World War One at a distance, from the French valley his mother's family came from. He was never inflamed by nationalist discourse about the "German mission." He signed up as a volunteer for the infantry reserve, but soon enough alleged a severe back pain that would keep him off the battlefield. He served the German army from a desk in Munich, censoring foreign propaganda.

More than defeat, he was stirred by the instability that followed war. In fact, World War I had sheltered him: from the refuge of an office at the General Command in Munich, he drafted his essay on political romanticism; he paraded through university classrooms, giving lectures; he left bachelorhood behind. The peace of defeat, on the other hand, disturbed him. The new republic soon crumbled into chaos. His promising career as a law professor suddenly became uncertain. The disconcerting nature of politics pained Schmitt, who feared both Bolshevik contagion and Nazi fanatics coming into power: he was afraid. Perhaps nostalgia welled up inside him for the

---

[4] In Balakrishnan, *op. cit.,* p. 13.

[5] Cited by Joseph W. Bendersky, *Carl Schmitt. Theorist for the Reich* (Princeton, New Jersey: Princeton University Press, 1983), p. 5.

past: the discipline and clarity imposed by war seemed, in his view, preferable to the turbulence of civil unrest. He therefore approached the institutions of the new republic by seeking a way to inject them with an ordering principle. During this period, he wrote his study on dictatorship: an argument in favor of extraordinary powers that would permit the rebuilding of peace.

Enter Mussolini. The March on Rome in October 1922 shook the apprehensive German lawyer to the core. From that day forward, Italian fascism wielded a powerful hold over him. He saw in that strength a potent movement that would launch the State into the conquest of the future, while at the same time saving the bourgeoisie from the threat of Communism. The door of history yet to come was thrown wide open: fascism offered a new rhetoric, new aesthetics, grandiose politics. The power of the masses –founding spark of an original State– dramatically unfolded during the fascists' march. Mussolini was daring: the violent deputy, whom so few had taken seriously, had called upon the king to impose order. Nothing had happened. And so he flooded the streets with black shirts and assumed control of the State. He gained his power by *displaying* it. Like a sand castle, the old regime crumbled at a single blow. A seductive myth was born: people on the move, guided by an energetic strongman, had taken over the State or, rather, had become the State. The old frontiers between society and State were diluted in this fusion of people and government in motion. "We have created our myth," Mussolini said following the success of the March, "That myth is a faith, it is passion. There is no need for it to become a reality. It is a reality because it is good, it is a hope, a faith, it is courage. Our myth is the Nation, our myth is the greatness of that Nation! And to this myth, to this grandeur we wish to transform into a complete reality, we subordinate everything else."[6]

Mussolini was Carl Schmitt's hero. Unlike the German dictator, Mussolini embodied a philosophy worthy of the name. Or at any rate, that's what he believed. Mussolini, the most vigorous European leader since the death of Lenin, was no caricaturized Caesar to Schmitt, but rather a charismatic leader who had mobilized a nation under a new faith. This was, no more and no less, what fascism was intended to be: an intense, undisputed conviction. Years later, he was granted an interview with the general of the shaven crown at the Palazzo Venezia, the 16th-century building that housed the embassy of the Venetian republic and would later become the general headquarters of the fascist State. *Il Duce* would give his most famous speeches from the balconies of that palace. The lawyer was captivated by the dictator. They spoke of the State as eternal, in contrast with the ephemeral nature of political parties. Schmitt told Mussolini that Hegel's historic legacy was in Rome. Not in Moscow, not in Berlin, but right there, in the Palazzo. Hegel, the man who had consecrated the State, lived on through the visionary musculature of the square-jawed totalitarian. This conversation would remain in Schmitt's memory as one of the greatest intellectual pleasures of his entire life, an unforgettable encounter, down to the last detail.

In 1927, the most polemic of Schmitt's works first saw the light of day: *The Concept of the Political.* Following

---

[6] Héctor Orestes Aguilar, *Carl Schmitt, teólogo de la política* (Mexico: Fondo de Cultura Económica, 2001), p. 73.

Machiavelli, Schmitt intended to look politics straight in the eye, without any moralistic beating around the bush. Few lines have captured the bellicose substance behind politics like this one from the second section of the essay: "The specific political distinction to which political actions and motives can be reduced is that between friend and enemy."[7] War is not the abyss into which politics might fall; war is the swamp from which politics emerges and can never escape. Social Democratic politician Ernst Niekish read *The Concept of the Political* as a bourgeois response to the Marxist theory of class struggle. Indeed, Schmitt was convinced, like Marx, that conflict was the motor of history; but unlike the materialist philosopher, he didn't attribute the passage of history to economic conflict. History, which could never free itself of politics, required the figure of the enemy and the engine of war. Such an enemy could be economic, racial, tribal, or national. Jacques Derrida has suggested that this fixed notion of enmity as the root of the political is derived from fear: the threat of the invisible, anguish over the enemy phantom. In one of his private notebooks, Schmitt reveals this quite clearly:

> Franz Kafka could have written a novel: the Enemy. Then it would have become clear that the indeterminacy of the enemy evokes anxiety (there is no other kind of anxiety, and it is the essence of angst to sense an indeterminate enemy; by contrast, it is a matter of reason (and in this sense of high

---

[7] I am citing the version of *The Concept of the Political* translated by George Schwab (Chicago, Illinois: University of Chicago Press, 2008).

> politics) to determine who is the enemy [...] and with this determination, the anxiety stops and at most fear remains.[8]

War sates the appetite of certainty. In battle, the phantom acquires a body: this is the real enemy, the one who must be annihilated. Our anguish fades the moment the enemy appears in our sights.

A year after the publication of his essay on the political, Schmitt joined the University of Berlin. There, at the heart of the Weimar Republic, he witnessed political paralysis, economic depression, mass unemployment, violence in the streets. Pluralism had become paralysis. Amid this milieu, the professor urgently defended the need for presidential empire. He argued that said demand fully complied with the rule of law. The president should be the true defender of the constitution –not the Supreme Court, as the liberals would have it. Here is where his complex relationship with power began. In times of crisis, Schmitt's reasoning resembled a life raft: the president should break through the parliamentary fence and assume dictatorial powers. He sustained that the Executive branch was at the core of the State. Let there be no doubt: the most important monopoly of all, the monopoly on arms, belonged exclusively to him.

Schmitt was an anti-liberal republican. He believed that the way to save the endangered republic was by making it more robust through greater leeway, not asphyxiating it with limitations. Moreover, he sustained that anti-constitutional parties (at the time, he meant communists

---

[8] See Jacques Derrida, *Politics of Friendship* (London: Verso, 1997).

and national socialists) should not be given the chance to destroy the republic. In 1930, he sustained that the State could not remain impassive before groups that were attempting to destroy it. Neutrality in the face of fanaticism was nothing less than suicidal.

Then he stumbled across Hitler. The notes in his journal on the eve of Nazi triumph show him to be anguished, bitter, saddened. The republic was dying out, and the triumph of fury seemed inevitable. As his most fortunate biographer has indicated, Schmitt may have expressed ideas that went against the rule of law in the strictest sense, but he never wished for the defeat of constitutional order. He certainly sympathized with the far right, but he imagined its possible fulfillment under a constitutional framework.[9] He was annoyed by Hitler's victory, but soon came to believe National Socialism could provide a solution to all the chaos. Hitler was determined to determine. That is why Schmitt embraced the new order. A combination of emotional and intellectual impulses had brought him closer to Nazisim. Ambition and opportunism must also have played a major role. Not to mention his certainty that the reigning chaos had goaded him into an alliance with anyone who would act as the executioner of liberalism.

It wasn't difficult to make his ideas jibe with the propaganda of the new regime. He merely found himself obliged to conceal a few journalistic articles. The rest of his work marched right along to fascist tunes. He did not have to alter his major texts in order to color them with Hitlerian rhetoric. The bellicose conceptualization of pol-

---

[9] See Chapter 12 of Balakrishnan's biography.

itics, the emphasis on executive coercion, and the mistrust of parliamentary deliberation and judicial neutrality all came out of his earlier writing. During the Nazi era, he simply projected those same ideas in order to outline a new legal philosophy. The jurist's affiliations continue to amaze us: Schmitt was Catholic, he had publicly opposed the Nazis. He was an outsider. But he had acquired prestige as an advocate of new ideas. That is why he was called upon to discuss a law that would legitimize the subordination of all political and social institutions to the dictates of the Party.

Soon thereafter, he was dubbed "crown jurist." In effect, as legal adviser, he defended all acts of the new regime. The nighttime murders with long knives, the bloody baptism of Hitlerian terror: all were applauded by Schmitt as dignified expressions of revolutionary justice. He revised his edition of *The Concept of the Political* in order to eliminate any references to Marxism and to incorporate the reigning vocabulary. His texts took on an anti-Semitic flair. In the most abject of these, he extolled Hitler as the architect of a new legality. All historical experience came to life through him; this gave him the strength and right to found a new order. The leader's acts were not subject to justice because they were, in and of themselves, the highest form of justice. No one more qualified than he to adjust the contents and limits of his own power, after all.[10]

Flattery would get him nowhere. Schmitt never actually held a relevant position in the upper echelons of

---

[10] Schmitt's text is anthologized in Héctor Orestes Aguilar's compilation as "El Führer defiende el derecho."

power. He was used up and discarded by the Nazi regime. It was not long before his judicial ingeniousness had become expendable. He would say years later that these were men who hated lawyers even more than they hated Jews: another major difference with Italian fascism, which coddled right-wing intellectuals. Besides, the men in uniform never fully accepted him. He was seen as a *marrano*, an unreliable convert. By 1934, he had started to draw criticism from the staunchest defenders of the regime. He was accused of ignoring the biological fundamentals of politics, of postulating a concept of Nationhood that was incompatible with the racial community defended by Hitler.[11] The star of the "crown jurist" had begun to fade. He had become suspect, a pariah. The local media summed up his choices: flee, or be sent to a concentration camp. Once again, Schmitt was living in fear. He stayed in Germany until the wave of attacks subsided. He lost his party privileges, but gained a certain degree of tranquility. From that point on, he opted for silence. Never again would he utter a single word about German politics. He took refuge in the field of international law, and kept to the shadows.

In 1945, the Russian army invaded Berlin and arrested Carl Schmitt in his home. He was to remain in jail for nearly two years. Robert Kempner, a lawyer who had emigrated from Germany, was in charge of interrogating him at Nuremberg. He was interested in learning whether Schmitt had any link to or complicity with the crimes of Nazism.

---

[11] See Bendersky's biography, p. 222.

Schmitt: That will always be the case when someone takes a position in such situations. I am an intellectual adventurer.

Kempner: You have the blood of an intellectual adventurer?

Schmitt: Yes, that is how thoughts and knowledge develop. I assume the risk. I have always accepted the consequences of my actions. I have never tried to avoid paying my bills.

Kempner: If, however, what you call the pursuit of knowledge results in the murder of millions of people?

Schmitt: Christianity also resulted in the murder of millions of people. One does not know unless one has experienced it oneself.

Schmitt ducked any moral considerations regarding his conduct. From that point on, he identified with Benito Cereno, one of Melville's main characters. A ship's captain, Cerreno is taken prisoner by slaves following a mutiny. The captain is forced by the rebels to guide them and steer the craft but in reality, he is a hostage, following his captors' orders. That is how Schmitt presented himself: intelligence abducted by tyranny.

Years later, he would write *Ex Captivitate Salus,* an autobiographical poem:

I have experienced the tribulations of fate.
Victories and defeats, revolutions and restorations.
Inflations and deflations, bombings,
Defamations, broken regimes and broken pipes,
Hunger and cold, internment and solitary confinement.
Through it all I have passed,
And through me it all has passed.

I am acquainted with the abundant varieties of terror,
The terror from above and the terror from below,
Terror on the land and terror from the air,
Terror legal and extra-legal,
Brown, red and checkered terror,
And worst of all, the terror none dares to name.
I am acquainted with them all and know their grip.

I know the chanting choirs of power and law,
The shrieking voices and mean falsifiers of the regime,
The black lists with many names.
And the cardfiles of the persecutors.

What now should I sing? The hymn of *placebo*?
Should I abandon problems and envy plants and animals?
Tremble in panic in the circle of the paniscs?
Fortunate as the gnat, who dances to his own tune? [...] [12]

Retired from public life, Carl Schmitt took on the task of his own vindication. Never again would he teach classes in German universities. The doors he once opened would remain closed to him forever. He returned to his hometown, Plettenberg. His refuge would be re-baptized San Cassiano. There were two reasons for this. On the one hand, the name referred to Machiavelli's refuge in times of disgrace, where he drafted all twenty-six chapters of *The Prince*. On the other, this German Catholic was well aware that the man of San Cassiano was a martyr, shot

[12] *Ex Captivitate Salus*, cited by Enrique Tierno Galván in *Revista de Estudios Políticos*, vol. xxxiv, year x, no. 54 (Madrid: 1950). English translation by G. L. Ulmen.

down by his own students with the very instruments he had taught them how to use.

San Cassiano became the capital of his vast epistolary republic. With great care, through hundreds of letters to European and American intellectuals, Carl Schmitt gradually built a broad network of correspondents to whom he attempted to justify his positions. Although the university and press were off limits, the post office continued to welcome him. And his home also welcomed visitors, who marveled at the generosity and pleasantness of the man who had tried to establish the "sovereignty of hatred."

As Jan Werner Müller indicates in a recent study, it is possible that no thinker from the 20th century enjoyed such a broad span of readers.[13] Interlocutor to Hannah Arendt, hero to sympathizers of Latin American dictatorships, ideologue of the Franco regime, inspiration to Italian Marxists and the new right wing of the late 20th century, required reading among student leaders of '68 and post-Marxist writers alike. Who could possibly equal the scope of his attraction?

Carl Schmitt's life may also be viewed through the spyglass of friendship. In Ernst Jünger, he found a travel companion for life. They met in 1930, in Berlin. Four years later, they were bosom buddies. When they first met, each was in his way a figure in German intellectual circles. Schmitt was recognized as an authority in the field

---

[13] *A Dangerous Mind. Carl Schmitt in Post-War European Thought* (New Haven, Connecticut: Yale University Press, 2003).

of jurisprudence and also as the author of polemic essays about Romanticism, the theological origins of emergency powers, and the irremediably bellicose nature of politics. Jünger, seven years younger than Schmitt, was enveloped in even greater fame. He wasn't just a talented writer: he was a war hero. They had a lot in common. Both of them were adventurers and loners. They shared concerns over Germany's fate and a fascination with war, myths, and books. But Jünger was more than a bookworm; he was a partisan with the kind of vital intensity that only experience can offer. He had joined the army in 1914 and been sent to the front in France, where he was wounded fourteen times and received the Pour le Mérite decoration for courage on the field of battle. *Storm of Steel,* the book he wrote while still in combat, became one of the classics of war literature. André Gide viewed it as the most beautiful book about war ever; a testimony beyond compare for its stylistic perfection, veracity, and forceful integrity.

Although his war portraits were admired by Hitler's followers and by the leader himself, he rejected the nationalist's plebeian demagoguery. It's been said that Goebbels offered him a post as delegate before the Nazis came into power. Jünger responded from the heights of poetic aristocracy that a good verse was worth more than the votes of eighty thousand idiots. At one point, he glorified war as an aesthetic experience. He was able to sense totalitarianism, he was a protégé of Hitler's, he never believed in liberal democracy. Having played with fire bound him closely to Schmitt. War put men on the brink of the precipice in a state of sublime excitation: the intoxication of a borderline scenario, the icy caress of the void, the escape from unbearable normality. “Grown up in an age of security, we shared a yearning for danger, for the experience of the extraordinary.”[14] War offered these great, strong, splendid things. The ecstasy of war could be compared to saintly entrancement, poetry, and love:

> Masculinity gets carried away by enthusiasm to the extent that the blood boils in one’s veins and in one’s heart. This is the mother of all intoxications, an unleashing that bursts all chains. A furor without consideration or barriers, comparable only to the violence of nature. Man is there, like the howling storm, the sea that roars and the thunder that bellows. There he blends into everything, he crashes against the dark gates of death like a shot on target. And the purpled waves engulf him in such a way that, for some time now, no awareness of the passage remains in him. It is as if a wave had dragged him back into the tempestuous sea.[15]

Waves that, once they had crashed, would reveal the true man. There, during “the dance of sharpened knives” along the thread that separates life from death, were revealed both man and his meaning: struggle. “Baptism by fire! The air was charged with such a surge of manhood that it made one want to cry, without knowing why.” The combatant in the trenches is marked by the anguished palpitation of uncertainty, the rumbling of his own death. War takes the soldier back to a time when life hung in the balance. Every thread of air penetrating the body is a divine

[14] *Storm of Steel* (New York: Penguin Books, 2004), p. 5.

[15] *La guerra como experiencia interior,* cited by Christian Graf von Krockow, *La decisión. Un estudio sobre Ernst Jünger, Carl Schmitt y Martin Heidegger* (Mexico: Ediciones Cepcom, 2001), p. 86.

gift, a don to be enjoyed as if it were the most exquisite wine. War is to Jünger, or at least to this Jünger of youthful journals, a mystical experience: a contact with the absolute that lends meaning to existence. It is also the most intense aesthetic experience. The fire of artillery is a wild, colorful dance in which flares are interspersed with white, black, and yellow clouds. Detonations, as Jünger wrote in the pages of his diary, are reminiscent of the canary's song.

Perhaps what Claudio Magris says about Jünger's treatment of the terrible is true. There is a kind of ostentation in his prose, a boast of cold blood.[16] At any rate, he didn't try to sugarcoat the disgraces of the century. One of his greatest sources of pride was his collection of beetles, which featured nearly 50,000 species. Perhaps the maximum tribute paid to him was the baptism of a butterfly in Pakistan with his name: *Trachydura jüngeri*. In the infinite world of insects, Jünger found a natural fantasia of jewels. Beetles, tiny beings with steely skin, embodied both the exquisite and the monstrous. The vast collector of coleopteri shut himself up in his studio, honed his gaze, and stopped to observe what was invisible, or repugnant, to others, taking down in great detail what his eyes registered. Men and insects, trapped alike in the unerring net of his gaze.

Jünger flirted early on with National Socialism but, once Hitler came into power, distanced himself from the Nazis and formed ties with opposition groups. In 1933, when Kniébolo (the name given to Hitler in his writings) came

---

[16]Claudio Magris, "Venerable sí, grande no," *El mundo* (Madrid: February 18, 1998).

into power, he moved out of Berlin. He opted for "retreat into the forest." He fled into the woods as a manifestation of his will to depend on no one other than himself.[17] Schmitt chose to go in the opposite direction. Having acted as an advisor to the last constitutional government and expressed his mistrust of the extremists, he threw himself into backing the new regime. During the Weimar period, Jünger had a brush with radical anti-Semitism, whereas Professor Schmitt sustained close relationships with Jewish colleagues and disciples. By the time Hitler had come into power, Jünger despised racism as a doctrine, whereas Schmitt attempted to portray himself as an exemplary anti-Semite.

These crossroads cast a cloud over the affection between the two bosom buddies, and yet the thread of their epistolary conversation was never broken. Jünger rejected Schmitt's collaboration with the fascists, but still encountered eroticism in his friend's intelligence. This he registered by talking to him. In his journal entry dated July 17, 1939, he noted the following:

> What has always caught my attention about C[arl] S[chmitt] is the good manufacture and order of his thoughts; they cause the impression of a power that is there, present, of a presential power. When he drinks he becomes even more alert, he sits there, immobile, a red flush on his face as if he were an idol [...] The endearing thing about Carl Schmitt, which brings us to love him, is that he is still capable of amazement despite having sur-

[17] "The retreat into the forest followed upon proscription. Through it a man asserted his will to survive by virtue of his own strength." *The Retreat into the Forest, Confluence, An International Forum*, vol. 3, issue 2 (1954), pp. 127-42.

> passed the age of fifty. Most people, and this happens early on in life, adopt a new fact only to the degree in which it guards some relationship with their system or interests. There is a lack of gusto for phenomena in and of themselves, or because of their diversity –a lack of the *eros* through which the spirit takes on a new impression, as it would take on a grain of seed.[18]

Schmitt and Jünger were brought together by another force: their sense of impending doom. Would they have to give up their dream of settling down and learn to slumber in the bosom of catastrophe? Calamity is the shadow that accompanies the world. Far from dispelling it, the lights of modernity make it loom even more darkly. During the intense epistolary exchange between the two friends, there is an image that reappears time and time again: that of the Titanic sinking into the icy waters of the Atlantic. Hobbes' primordial passion, Fear, was symptomatic of modernity according to both men. Progress and panic collided against the ruined hull of the Titanic, as did comfort and destruction, engineering and disaster. Such are our lives.

Any approach to Carl Schmitt's thought should take style into account. Schmitt's prose is far from academic. Distanced from the detachment of Weber, his mentor; far removed from the rigorous dryness of his abhorred intellectual nemesis, Kelsen; Schmitt wrote with the forcefulness of an erudite man and the zeal of a pamphleteer; the ambition of a theorist and the magic of an aphorist. His phrases swing

[18] Ernst Jünger, *Radiaciones. Diarios de la Segunda Guerra Mundial* (Barcelona: Tusquets, 1995), pp. 56-57.

back and forth between lawyerly detail and esoteric abstraction. In his prose, speech is not a vehicle used to transport thoughts gratuitously. Style frequently hijacks reason, or better yet, seduces it, using it to envelop the reader. Schmitt's feverish prose, as Stephen Holmes indicates, imprints words with such drama, that any constitutional technicality becomes capable of determining the destiny of man.[19]

Like Hobbes, Carl Schmitt understood that political reflection couldn't be merely a science; above all, it was an action. Making the world of power intelligible through words is the same as remaking it. Hobbes' case is revealing. His *Leviathan* is an attempt to establish order by crafting definitions. If war is confusion, peace is to be found in the voice of clarity. War arises from a struggle for words, an absence of shared meanings, a vacuum of understanding. Therefore, in Hobbes' philosophy, metaphor is an unacceptable fraud. And yet we find that the sage of Malmesbury is, together with Plato, the most prolific creator of political imagery. One need go no further than the monster that lends its name to his classic treatise, and whose figure appears on the frontispiece of his work. Hobbes was compelled to draw allegories from power, law, and man. Such is the curse of metaphor. Not even those who have declared war on it can break free from its power.

Schmitt's dictionary is a veritable art collection. Allegories parade across the length and breadth of his writing. His portrayal of politics is a canvas representing war between enemies. The sovereign is portrayed as the man who

---

[19] Stephen Homes, *The Anatomy of Antiliberalism* (Cambridge, Massachusetts: Harvard University Press, 1993).

remains standing when all else has failed: one who rules by exception. Democracy is the body that melds the governing with the governed. Constitution becomes the power of decision. Liberalism, the cowardice of merchants, the babbling of polemicists, the entertainment of brutes. As this collection shows, Schmitt does not assemble concepts using the resources of logic; he renders images through the enchantments of metaphor. Great painters, he writes, not only show beautiful things, they express a conscience that puts everything in its place: an eye here, an arm there; blue over this way, green a bit further down: "the true painter is a man who sees things and people better and with more precision than other men, with greater exactitude, moreover, in the sense of the historic reality of his time."[20] This was Carl Schmitt's ambition: to become the great painter of power, the political conscience of his time.

Allow me to focus on that first image: the political. This is, beyond a doubt, the central nervous system of Carl Schmitt's political theory. All of his thought springs from the lines of *The Concept of the Political* and returns, sooner or later, to those same paragraphs. It first appeared in September 1927, as an article of just thirty-three pages. In time, it would grow; but not much. Even after his final revision in 1963, it continued to be a brief essay: a portable bomb. It is Jünger who first noted the explosive character of this text: "a mine that silently explodes." The detonation comes in the essay's second section: "the specific political distinction to which political actions

---

[20] Carl Schmitt, *Tierra y mar. Consideraciones sobre la historia* universal (Madrid: Estudios políticos, 1952), pp. 71-72.

and motives can be reduced is that between friend and enemy."[21] If an essential distinction between good and evil is drawn on moral terrain, or if we are allowed to distinguish between beauty and ugliness within the realm of aesthetics, then the political domain is constituted by a distinction between friend and foe. Friendship and enmity can be derived from any human walk of life. The difference becomes political once it has been intensified to the utmost degree. Conflict acquires this nature once it has turned unavoidably antagonistic: annihilation of the enemy becomes a condition for survival. Conflict has reached an extreme, there can be no third party that intervenes in order to reconcile positions, there are no valid rules. The enemies are at war.

As the cliché goes: life is struggle. But the political dimension of this clash is no vague representation of an effort to overcome resistance; it is nothing more and nothing less than a conflict that could lead to death: "The friend, enemy, and combat concepts receive their real meaning precisely because they refer to the *real possibility of physical killing*." Let us call politics, then, the most radical of oppositions between men: an opposition marked by the shadow of death.

But, as Giovanni Sartori correctly points out, Schmitt's argument lacks proof. Despite its Hobbesian drama, *The Concept of the Political* is a worm devouring its own tail. His is, in effect, a circular argument: "everything that regroups into friend-enemy is political; everything that does not regroup in this manner isn't, and that which is po-

---

[21] *The Concept of the Political, op. cit.*, p. 56.

litical voids out that which is not political."[22] Schmitt, driven by the illusion of constructing a more pure political theory, attempts to capture its elemental atom, to hunt down its essence. The problem is that in his search for the nucleus, he winds up losing a great deal of the matter at hand. Any consensus, any agreement, any conciliation is written off as anti-political. As Sartori accurately observes, Schmitt speaks only of "hot politics," while ignoring "cold politics" completely. Given the combative side of politics, the no less important element of consensus is raised. Machiavelli, who also had a taste for metaphor and myth, portrayed politics as a centaur: half man, half beast. There can be no state without an army, no politics without violence. But neither can there be politics of pure violence, pure conflict, pure enmity. Politics without conflict is just as false as politics of nothing but conflict.

While flawed in logical and methodological terms, Schmittian evocation is powerful. Schmitt was well aware of this. In *Political Romanticism* he cites the Italian poet Giovanni Papini: "wherever we are concerned with phenomena on a grand scale and with colossal movements, nothing is more precise than a vague word."[23] The political precision of conceptual vagueness. Schmitt understood concepts to be darts for the struggle rather than precision instruments. Any concept, Schmitt wrote, has a polemic meaning: it is born in opposition to a concrete antagonism. The words of politics are meaningless if one

---

[22] Giovanni Sartori, "Política," in *Elementos de una teoría política* (Madrid: Alianza Editorial, 1992), p. 220.

[23] Papini, *El crepúsculo de los filósofos,* cited in *Political Romanticism* (Cambridge, Massachusetts: MIT Press, 1986), p. 7.

doesn't understand against whom one is fighting. Therefore, it is worthwhile for us to question the polemic significance of his image of the political.

One thing is obvious: politics are born out of a need to refute the anti-political. But, where does the anti-political reside? In liberalism. The Schmittian notion of the political is a vessel into which he poured his anti-liberal fury. Liberalism, according to Schmitt, ignores politics. It takes refuge in ethical judgments and economic calculations. Under this canopy, there are no enemies or decisions to be made: there are only partners, adversaries, and competitors. Liberalism doesn't call for a definition. It is the realm of impersonal mechanisms: law, market, debate. Justice is expressed by general rules, price is naturally determined by competition, truth is illuminated through free exchange. But there are no conflicts, no tough decisions. Thus politics are negated. Where José Ortega y Gasset encounters the noble generosity of liberalism (the will to live with one's enemy), Schmitt sees only cowardice, emptiness.

Carl Schmitt's essay about the political, rather than the didactic exploration of a word, turns out to be a harsh pamphlet decrying liberalism. Here, sharply outlined, we find the causes underlying his abomination: the liberals' bourgeois horizon turns the world into a business proposition, transforming politics into idle chatter, enhancing the cowardice of indecision. Trapped within this icy liberal machinery, men spend their meaningless lives in a mild, mediocre fashion that lacks purpose. After all, Schmitt was a big admirer of Tocqueville, whom he doesn't hesitate to rank as the greatest historian of the 19th century. A man with a sweet, clear, and perpetually sorrowful gaze, Tocqueville was a "vanquished man accepting his defeat." The anti-liberal extolling the giant from the opposite camp; the mystic decision-maker honoring the Hamlet of politics. If Tocqueville was admired by Schmitt, it is because the *vanquished one* was able to see liberalism from the vacuum that it was. Therein lies the genius of his poignant eye.

If we lack a life-reaffirming enemy, we vegetate aimlessly. The tragedy of politics arises thus from a hunger for meaning. The struggle that threatens our survival lends meaning to the world: us vs. them; good vs. evil; friend vs. foe. Man is in need of causes that can pick him up off the ground, saturate him with emotion, add gravity to his existence. Man needs to confront the seriousness of life. To Schmitt, this describes the human inclination toward tragedy. Only in the struggle with one's mortal enemy does life appear in all its glory, in all its gravity. This was best described by Theodor Däubler, Schmitt's friend, in a poem:

> The enemy is our own question as a figure.
> And he will hunt us, and we him, to the same end.[24]

This interrogation of ourselves points towards the body of all those who threaten our survival. The mechanics of the political turns out, thus, to be constituent of individuality. In order to become human, we must heed the dilemmas that defy us: good or evil, us or them, God or

[24] In Heinrich Meier, *The Lesson of Carl Schmitt* (Chicago, Illinois: The University of Chicago Press, 1998), p. 44. Here, I am following Meier's interpretation regarding the theological characteristics of Schmitt's political philosophy.

Satan. These choices lie at the root of politics. The idea of original sin is crucial to Schmitt's political theology. The world of men can be broken down into primordial enmities. The enmity to which we are condemned is a consequence of original sin. It says so in the book of Genesis, "I will put enmity between you and the woman, and between your seed and her seed." Out of disobedience, humanity is no longer one: man has become an enemy of man. Humanity is no more. Schmitt said as much, echoing De Maistre's old adage, "whoever invokes humanity wants to cheat."[25] The zoological label of humanity is an imposition, because the descendants of Adam live in irremediable hostility. And man is incapable of attaining reconciliation. Only through God can there be humanity. In the meantime: war. Politics.

Carl Schmitt celebrated his fiftieth birthday by paying tribute to Thomas Hobbes. On his birthday, July 11, 1938, he wrote the preface to his essay on the *Leviathan.* My cellmate after the fall of Hitler, he said, was Thomas Hobbes. Indeed, Schmitt has been called "the Hobbes of the 20th century." But the comparison is faulty. In their anthropological pessimism, their recognition of fear as the main drive behind politics, their appeal for the conformation of unrestricted power, their hatred for pluralism, and their decisionism, the two thinkers coincide. Schmitt always referred to the author of the *Leviathan* with admiration, describing him in the first edition of his

[25] "The concept of humanity is an especially useful ideological instrument of imperialist expansion, and in its ethical-humanitarian form it is a specific vehicle of economic imperialism," in *The Concept of the Political, op. cit.,* p. 83.

Concept of the Political as the greatest and perhaps only truly systematic political thinker. At the end of the day, Schmitt personally identified with the legend of Hobbes. We shall be engulfed in the same shadow, he predicted. Terror joined the destinies of Schmitt and Hobbes. The acidity of fear is present in both their inks. But many theoretical dimensions lay between them. While it is true that they both viewed the problem of politics through the optics of power and articulated reasons to edify an imposing force, it is also true that they did so with diametrically opposed goals. Thomas Hobbes feeds his monster in order to keep the peace. Carl Schmitt, on the contrary, seeks a State that will militarize society. In Hobbesian theory, hope is kindled that the State will soothe politics, that conflict will be frozen under state sovereignty. In Schmittian theory, the possibility that this tranquility could come to pass is passionately refuted. In Schmittian terms, Hobbes is the most anti-political of political theoreticians because he dreams of the tranquility of a pacifying State: he is an absolutist of liberal fiber. Hobbes, in effect, projects an artifact of peace to allow the flourishing of a quiet life, commerce, science, and art. The pact through which civilization is established.

To Schmitt, this world without conflict is a meaningless circus, a carnival not to be taken seriously. Peace is necessary for survival, Hobbes says; war is necessary for true existence, Schmitt would respond. The State, according to Schmitt, lends meaning to death: it is the instance that demands sacrifice. One of the sharpest readers of Schmitt, Leo Strauss, has described these opposing forces quite well: "Whereas Hobbes in an unliberal world accomplishes the founding of liberalism, Schmitt in a liberal world undertakes the critique of liberalism."[26]

Schmitt would describe his anti-liberalism as democratic. Democracy marches on, triumphantly. And the opportunist's realism imposes itself. Democracy, Schmitt sustained, is essentially anti-liberal. The lawyer insists on this antagonism: democracy is the identity between governing and governed. It necessarily presupposes homogeneity. "A democracy demonstrates its political power by knowing how to refuse or keep at bay something foreign and unequal that threatens its homogeneity." Democracy excludes all that is foreign, while liberalism attempts to reconcile it: an insurmountable contradiction "between liberal notions of human equality and democratic homogeneity."[27] The Schmittian notion of democracy is clearly anti-liberal, anti-pluralistic, and anti-constitutional. A Rousseauian blend, no less. Carl Schmitt, the Rousseau of the 20th century?

Upon writing his essay on parliamentarism in 1923, Schmitt argued that representative government was on its deathbed. It had become a mask. Its intellectual fundamentals –public deliberation and the balance of power– were out of touch with reality. Modern parliamentarism had not ended secrecy, nor had it managed to disperse

---

[26] The analysis by Strauss of Schmitt's work can be read in Heinrich Meier, *Carl Schmitt and Leo Strauss. The Hidden Dialogue* (Chicago, Illinois: The University of Chicago Press, 1995), p. 102.

[27] Carl Schmitt, "On the contradiction between Parliamentarism and Democracy," in *Crisis of Parliamentary Democracy (Studies in Contemporary German Social Thought)* (Cambridge, Massachusetts: MIT Press, 2000), p. 15.

power. It perversely blocked any identification between government and society. Therefore, the only way to reconstitute a democratic regime was by purging it of its liberal traits. Freedom of the press, the secret ballot, the right to assembly of the opposition, and the autonomy of social groups were liberal bacilli destroying the "emotional unity" of democracy. Dictatorship was the authentic vehicle of popular unity. Its expression was the will of the people, expressed by acclamation. Thus, no cry was more democratic than the "We are all *il Duce*" of Italian fascism. Full identity. Thus fascism, Bolchevism, Caesarism are certainly anti-liberal, but not anti-democratic. Quite the contrary.

Schmitt's democratism is also deeply anti-constitutional. The author of *Constitutional Theory* was always fascinated by the exceptional, the unorganized, and the irregular: the untamed. The normal territory of politics is crisis. One cannot aspire to the domestication of politics. It cannot ever be submitted to fixed rules. Its rock bottom is abnormality. The charm of the exceptional can be gleaned from his idea of sovereignty, but above all, from his conceptualization of law and State.

According to Schmitt, it is neither possible nor desirable for society to be ordered according to general rules. Law applies to the ordinary state of things. But in politics, normality isn't normal. Hence Schmitt's *juridical situationism*. The need is imposed to decide case by case in keeping with the demands of the moment. Concrete measures before general laws. The fundamentals of Schmitt's decisionism can be found in the thought of Spanish author Donoso Cortés. Indeed, he was one of the German lawyer's favorite writers. Off to one side of the Hobbesian philosophical platform, Cortés' passionate speeches and essays emerge as the pulpit from which Schmitt's reasoning is preached. Cortés is also an emergency thinker, one who denounces the failure of enlightened ideals. Power is founded on decision, not calculation or norms. Therefore, norms must be subordinated to the imperative of resolute will. "[L]aws are made for societies, not societies for laws. I say: society, everything through society, everything for society; always society, society in all circumstances and on all occasions. When the letter of the law is enough to save a society, then the letter of the law is best." In the event of confusion, there is no alternative to dictatorship. If anything, there is a choice of dictatorships: "One must choose between a dictatorship that comes from below and one that comes from above. I choose the one from above because it comes from the most clean and serene regions. Finally, one must choose between a dictatorship of the dagger and a dictatorship of the saber. I choose the dictatorship of the saber because it is more noble." The Spanish parliamentarian himself anticipated the porous notion of constitutionality that would later be defended by Nazism's ephemeral advocate. A constitution had to make room for its own infraction. God himself was the great master of shattered constitutionality. Cortés sustained that the Creator governs constitutionally, and "[t]here are some direct, clear, and specific times when he manifests his sovereign will by breaking the laws he himself has imposed, thereby bending the natural course of things. So, gentlemen," he concluded, addressing the Courts, "when God operates this way, can it not be said, if human language can be applied to divine things, that he is operating dictatorially?"[28]

Schmitt's decisionism leads directly to an anti-normative interpretation of the constitution. Schmitt cannot accept that constitutional materials are legal binds. A constitution is not a norm, but a decision. Therefore, legal positivism practices a fetishism of sorts. It adores the object without understanding its contents. In order to surpass this limitation, one must scrutinize the true constitutional body; i.e., political decision. Thus Schmitt disavows the basic principle of constitutional thought: subjugation of power to law, limitation of power, depersonalization of power. In other words, he denies the possibility of legally domesticating power. Thus, political imperatives are treated as law.[29] The salvation of the State will always come before legal technicalities.

It wouldn't be long before constitutional politicization denaturalized this device. Paradoxically, the politicized constitution falls apart; that is to say, it becomes depoliticized. Schmitt, who considered himself first and foremost a jurist, managed to construct a jurisprudence for unlawfulness. A legal science that transformed law into a flimsy fabric, incapable of detaining power. Or rather: a wrapper to conceal its caprice. Politics is, according to Schmitt,

---

[28] Juan Donoso Cortés, trans. Jeffrey P. Johnson, "Speech on Dictatorship," in *Selected Works of Juan Donoso Cortés: (Contributions in Political Science)* (Connecticut: Greenwood Publishing Group, 2000), pp. 46, 57, and 48.

[29] As Germán Gómez Orfanel proposes in *Excepción y normalidad en el pensamiento de Carl Schmitt* (Madrid: Center of Constitutional Studies, 1986). Ignacio de Otto, in his *Derecho constitucional, sistema de fuentes* (Barcelona: Ariel, 1991) argues that the variety of concepts of constitution developed by Schmitt is so vast and disorienting that "it can only be explained as the result of the conscious attempt to deny the supremacy of the Constitution itself." The painter no longer draws images: he blows smoke.

inescapably wild. There is no room for regulation, because the ground is never stable. Politics is a carpet of upheavals. The State is governed by the unforeseeable, the unregulatable. Therefore, we will not find in his work any effort to build principles of institutional engineering. In his view, there isn't any way to raise solid constitutional structures, since the ground of politics is never firm. If politics is always a slippery slope, the State cannot be backboned with rules. Any other way of thinking would be to live in simple bliss, like a gnat dancing to its own tune.

Governing from a Bicycle Seat

> The purely logical spirits –the dialectical ones– are the most harmful. Existence is already in and of itself enormously illogical and miraculous. Many ripe, robust institutions have been caught up and destroyed in the syllogistic, perfect, vile gears of *ergo*ist lawyers. Free us, gods, from these theorizing, fanatical, straight-and-narrow insects that annihilate life.
>
> Julio Torri

The bicycle is a marvel of engineering. A two-wheeled vehicle that causes the person riding it to move forward, the bicycle is also an example of why technical rationale is faulty. A manual can teach you the manner in which the parts comprising it are pieced together: wheels, chain, pedals, frame, handlebars, seat, brakes. But no set of instructions can teach you how to ride one. The *Espasa Encyclopedia* quoted by Gabriel Zaid offers a prudent suggestion: "In order to ride a bicycle, it is necessary to be unafraid, grasping the handlebars loosely and looking straight ahead, not at the ground." Good advice, but we can hardly hope to succeed after this one, brief lesson. If we want to learn how to ride, nothing beats climbing on, starting to pedal and trying to maintain our balance while still in motion. Practice makes perfect. Skill can be acquired only through habit. Only by pedaling will you find your center, only by mounting can we learn to navigate our own weight. It would be foolish to assume cyclists are trained by reading thick volumes on the history and design of bicycles. A general theory of cycling isn't required reading for the competitors of the Tour de France. A cyclist's intelligence lies in his muscles; his wisdom, in his reflexes. This is the argument brandished by Michael Oakeshott against what he calls the rationalist "contagion" of politics. In order to govern, one must debunk the superstition of those who believe that politics is nothing more than the application of theory.

Michael Oakeshott was born in 1901. His father –an agnostic public official and friend to George Bernard Shaw– passed down a deep admiration for Montaigne that would accompany him always. Like the Father of the Essay, Oakeshott spent an entire lifetime wandering from one theme to the next. He drafted unmemorable theological reflections, wrote a philosophical essay on the idea of experience, published various studies on Hobbes, edited an anthology of contemporary European doctrines and, during the beehive of wartime, coauthored a slim volume on horseracing. How frivolous, his critics were quick to claim. While England bleeds, while freedom is being threatened around the world, the Professor dedicates himself to writing a manual for placing bets at the racetrack. But Oakeshott wasn't scratching his head at the library. He had enlisted in the army and was also, in his own way, doing battle through his texts. His work on contemporary political thought is an interesting document, written at a time of over-glorified ideologies when it would seem that all action ought to be lifted up in the name of a Great Idea. There were no movements that could not be shielded behind a vast, well-polished doctrine. Opportunism, he wrote in his introduction, had been castrated under the guise of principle. We had lost, Oakeshott lamented,[1] *the innocence of Machiavelli.* Machiavellian innocence: a fresh gaze that alights upon State affairs without the slightest scientific pretense in order to learn from history, rather than trying to teach it a lesson.

In 1947, he published what would become his most well known work: *Rationalism in Politics*, an essay that justly demolished the fundamentals of ideological politics. Halfway through the century –at the peak of his own existence– the London School of Economics invited him to head a Political Science faculty orphaned by Harold Laski's death. Laski embodied everything Oakeshott repudiated. The socialist professor saw the State as an instrument of social regeneration and believed in the muscular capabilities of politics. He lived under the illusion of intelligence: if Reason came into power, it would manage to set everything right. The contrast between Laski and his successor couldn't have been greater. Laski was an orator. The fiery words of this Laborist ideologue were always aimed at the burning issues of the day. His seminars were calls to action. Oakeshott's was another era. He wasn't terribly interested in current events. He could go for quite some time without reading the newspaper. The mania of

---

[1] *The Social and Political Doctrines of Contemporary Europe* (Cambridge: Cambridge University Press, 1939).

finding out about the news every day is a mental disorder, he would say. Above all, he had enough good taste to abhor oratory. Parrot-like eloquence was as much of an execrable practice to Professor Oakeshott as it was to the Mexican miniaturist whose signature accompanies this chapter's epigraph. The intellectual Julio Torri was referring to the antipathy he felt for those people who always struggle in the name of high-sounding causes, those vain individuals who read in order to capture quotes, not to gain understanding, and who speak in order to adulate or move the public, not to communicate.[2]

The London School of Economics was in and of itself a strange place for a philosopher like Oakeshott. The LSE was founded to educate a new political class under the idea that science –especially, as its name indicates, economic science– would successfully establish a prosperous, just, well organized society. Invoking a Positivist hymn of sorts, the founders of the London School of Economics would pray: "the facts will set us free." Students arrived at school searching for tools to rationally piece society back together again –which was precisely what Oakeshott thought education could not and should not teach them. Like a pacifist at a military academy, Oakeshott was an anti-rationalist in the congregation of Reason.

After introducing himself to the LSE students, he read a text that shook those student social engineers to the core. It seemed ungrateful, Oakeshott said in his message, that Harold Laski should be followed by someone

---

[2] See Torri's essay on the opposition of oratory temperament to artistic temperament in his *De fusilamientos* (Mexico: Fondo de Cultura Económica, 1964).

like him, "...a skeptic: one who would do better if only he knew how."

Unlike mechanics, politics isn't a technique, he warned them. It's rather more like cooking. No recipe book, no matter how complete it is or how clear its illustrations, will do any good to someone without a talent for seasoning. If you want to make duck confit, you've got to head for the kitchen, not the library. Philosophy may help us understand history, but it won't provide useful advice for governing. He called upon his students in this inaugural lecture to understand what he called the *intimations of tradition*. Submerging oneself in history was indispensable in order to vaccinate oneself against the smallpox of political optimism, thus ending once and for all the fairy tale that sees politics as the road that will lead us to a humble abode where we'll all live happily ever after. Laski's disciples were aghast.

Oakeshott was a solitary figure, a philosopher without followers. He shunned the public spotlight and was fairly determined not to form a school of thought. He feared his ideas would degenerate into ideology. That's why he struggled against the seductiveness of formulas: one who knows only the abbreviated version of things ignores all. There are no shortcuts to understanding Hobbes: he must be read. Oakshott's philosophical style –for his thought is, above all else, a *style*– does not fit into fashionable pigeonholes. He was a traditionalist with very few traditional ideas, a skeptical idealist, a man who loved freedom but was bored by liberal preaching. As Robert Grant (one of his few portraitists) said, Oakeshott was too indifferent to hierarchies and lineages to be followed by the Tories, too skeptical to be backed by the moralists, too liberal to be seconded by the right-wing populists. Oakeshott's voice is unique. Someone once called him the Proust of political science.

His friends say he was always accompanied by beautiful women. He boasted countless romances and only three weddings. One of his most intense affairs was with Iris Murdoch, the prolific Irish novelist and thinker. They met in Oxford in the late 1940s. Oakeshott was nearly twenty years her senior. He was an authority in his field; she was a radiant girl who had been militant in the Communist Party and exposed to some of the great minds of the century: Wittgenstein, Sartre, Canetti. In October 1950, they fell deeply in love. She wrote in her diary:

> Can't work or eat, just want to wander around thinking about M. What is he thinking today? I must try to work. I am making myself sick with emotion.
>
> *Later.* Feeling perfectly demented about M. I don't know how I can get through today without seeing him. Yet I can't decently call upon him again before tomorrow.[3]

Their affair was as intense as it was short-lived. Two months after it had begun, they parted ways: he'd fallen in love with another woman. Twenty years later, Iris Murdoch still remembered their fling, that morning when he kissed her feet. How beautiful she had felt then! Oakeshott's fol-

[3] Iris Murdoch's diary, quoted by Peter J. Conradi in his biography *Iris. The Life of Iris Murdoch* (New York: Norton, 2002), p. 312.

lowers were convinced that her relationship with him had inspired a character in one of her early novels. They were referring to Hugo Belfounder, an unclassifiable philosopher in *Under the Net,* the novel Murdoch published in 1954. A conversationalist of paused speech and endless questions; a man interested in everything, who sought a theory for everything. No: not a theory for everything, but rather a theory for *every* thing.

> During the early part of my discussions with Hugo I kept trying to "place" him. Once or twice I asked him directly whether he held this or that general theory – which he always denied with the air of one who has been affronted by a failure of taste. And indeed it seemed to me later that to ask such questions of Hugo showed a peculiar insensitivity to his unique intellectual and moral quality. After a while I realized that Hugo held no general theories whatsoever. All his theories, if they could be called theories, were particular.[4]

There are those who say that Iris Murdoch's character was a portrayal not of Oakeshott, but of Ludwig Wittgenstein or one of his disciples. This could be true. He is probably a literary composite of them all. But this reluctance to form a general theory, this aversion to any classifying mania that attempts to compress diversity, is clearly Oakeshottian. Oakeshott was possessed by the *intuition of the unique.* Following the Aristotelian route of classification is to deny the universe contained in every leaf on a tree, in every insect in the jungle. Theory, according to George

---

[4] Iris Murdoch. *Under the Net* (New York: Penguin Books, 1960), p. 58.

Steiner, is nothing more than perception losing its patience.[5] And Oakeshott was never in a hurry.

Flirtatious, well read, an exquisite conversationalist with a genius for gesture and detail, Oakeshott was the model English gentleman. In his final years, he decided to leave his apartment in Covent Garden a few blocks away from the London School of Economics in order to settle down in the small town of Acton, in Wessex. His cabin had neither telephone nor central heating, but it did have a chimney and a view of the sea. Beyond the curtains: the English Channel. There, in a slate house chock-full of books, Oakeshott lived out his final years reading, cooking, and tending to his garden. Joys of patience, labors that are, at the same time, solitary and generous, physical and spiritual acts. Cooking and gardening symbolically condense a political philosophy that refracts impatience, a philosophy consecrated to caressing its materials while attending to their gentle transformations.

On December 19, 1990, a week after turning eighty-eight, Michael Oakeshott died in bed. The *Daily Telegraph* would publish the following obituary a few days later: "Michael Oakeshott, who has died aged 89, was the greatest political philosopher in the Anglo-Saxon tradition since Mill - or even Burke." On the morning of December 24, he was buried on the Dorset coast. He would have liked his funeral, a friend of his commented: there was nothing extraordinary about it.

---

[5] George Steiner, *Errata* (New Haven, Connecticut: Yale University Press, 1998).

ACCORDING TO OAKESHOTT, RATIONALISTS ARE THOSE who, having projected ideas onto a plane, try to impose them on history; those who believe that politics consists of putting an outline into practice. Rationalists are those who drafted the *Declaration of Rights of Man and of the Citizen*, and the authors of the *Communist Manifesto* as well; utilitarian engineers and fascist demagogues. Rationalists are theologians who know everything about God and His creation of the world, and they are also terrorists who want to burn it all down in the name of infinite justice. Nationalist fables and economic equations. Of course, the English philosopher isn't waging a battle against reason, or advocating –as Rousseau did with cloying sentimentality– a return to sweet, innocent ignorance. Perhaps the brush he wields is too thick to caricaturize his adversary: any exercise of theoretical reflection that strays from experience is viewed with suspicion, and any attempt at philosophical invention in order to understand or modify political reality is discarded.[6] Locke's rationalism is saved from the sledgehammer thanks to the fact that it is a theory drenched in history; experience enunciated with a rationalist vocabulary. Oakeshott suggests that according to Locke's idea of natural rights, there is no invention, only memory. The rationalist infection, therefore, did not affect the Father of English Constitutionalism's marrow of reasoning, and only slightly, his form of expression. It did, however, affect his readers: in the United States and France his work was misread as a discourse

---

[6] See the essay on Oakeshott in Bhiku Parekh, *Pensadores políticos contemporáneos* (Madrid: Alianza Universidad, 1986).

of abstractions, awaiting the bayonets that would put it into practice. But it wasn't that: far from being the preface to future freedom, the *Second Treatise of Civil Government* was an epilogue to English habits.

The Rationalist whom Oakeshott criticizes wishes to live each day as if it were his first. He has a nonsensical aversion to habit, believing that all custom is erroneous, that nothing is worthy unless it has been tested in the laboratory of reason.

> To the Rationalist, nothing is of value merely because it exists (and certainly not because it has existed for many generations), familiarity has no worth, and nothing is to be left standing for want of scrutiny. And his disposition makes both destruction and creation easier for him to understand and engage in, than acceptance or reform. To patch up, to repair (that is, to do anything which requires a patient knowledge of the material), he regards as waste of time; and he always prefers the invention of a new device to making use of a current and well-tried expedient. He does not recognize change unless it is a self-consciously induced change, and consequently he falls easily into the error of identifying the customary and the traditional with the changeless.[7]

If the Rationalist's task consists of drawing up plans so that they may be later imposed upon reality, first off, he must clear his workspace of any old papers, family photographs, or remains of coffee and dessert left over from the night before. No souvenirs, no affections can be allowed to sully the rationalist plane. Geometry must be traced on a clean

---

[7] *Rationalism in Politics* (London: Metheun, 1962), p. 8.

slate. The design of reason must procure to "free our minds from old beliefs, old prejudices." That is why Plato is, aside from being the grandfather of the historicists abhorred by Karl Popper, the ancestor of the Rationalists Oakeshott loathed.[8] This poet, who was willing to annihilate all those older than age ten in order to raise a city unstained by corrupt habits, intended to make society a "blank sheet of infinite possibility." Whitewashing the mantle of history in search of utopia constitutes a will to exterminate. By rationalist calculations, there are always a few million spare human beings.

But the Rationalist is unaware of the fact that politics descends from ritual, not syllogism. The lessons of experience, therefore, make better playbooks than the recipes of ideology. Certainly Oakeshott saw in statism the great threat of his time, yet anti-Statists were not spared his criticism. Like planners, market idolizers believe the world entire should surrender to the formulas on their blackboards. A plan to eliminate any planning whatsoever expresses the exact same political style they had intended to transcend. His critique targets State devotees and market fanatics alike. Leninists and Thatcherians have more in common than it would seem: they are both heartless experiments. Plans convinced of their own dogma, deaf to reality's reply. The Polish political guru Adam Przeworski has shown a parallel between these categorical projects. Substitute "nationalization of the means of production"

---

[8] Popper, by the way, saw a "really original thinker" in Oakeshott but naturally wouldn't accept his blow against rationalism. See "Three views concerning human knowledge," in *Conjectures and Refutations. The growth of scientific knowledge* (New York and London: Routledge, 1963), p. 102.

with "privatization," and "planning" with "free enterprise," and we're left with a remarkably similar ideological structure.[9] Both radically condemn the past, both postulate a privileged historical subject, both believe they are privy to a technique that will subdue reality, and both require major surgery. They may change the ingredients, but the pastry is the same. Which path to take is the least of their concerns: in politics, all that matters is style.

Oakeshott points out the vagaries of proud reason. Incidentally, he doesn't offer up sentiment as an antidote. Emotions will not save us from these technological tongs. The only way out is through trial and error. We rehearse in order to learn the effects of every attempt, feeling our way tentatively before we squeeze, observing without pontificating, listening before and after we speak and then listening again, walking unhurriedly and aimlessly, pondering each step. The straight line is the path of the devil who, as we are well aware, is always in a hurry. Fortune, as Machiavelli stated in his *Discourses,* favors the agile.

In *The Politics of Faith and the Politics of Scepticism,* Oakeshott masterfully defends this trial-and-error policy. The purpose of politics is neither truth, nor perfection, nor beauty. The task of government is merely to diminish human conflict. Political order is always a precarious, superficial order. Underneath the tranquil surface of the State there will inevitably be conflict. Because we are always threatened by decadence, we must arm doubt with pessimism. Henry James called this propensity "the imagination of disaster."

---

[9] On this parallel between Leninism and Thatcherism, see Adam Przeworski, "The Neoliberal Fallacy," *Journal of Democracy*, vol. 3, no. 3 (July 1992).

From Oakeshott's skepticism emerges the quest for restricted, closely supervised government. That is why he has been called the liberals' favorite conservative.[10] According to Paul Franco, one of the first meticulous interpreters of his political philosophy, Oakeshott was a liberal who simply didn't like the last three letters in the word liberalism. Thus, it's no wonder that one of his favorite authors was an engineer of institutions: Benjamin Constant, the mechanic of political moderation. The path of rules and regulation, the weight of precedent, and the balance of discretion are vital to the bicyclist's journey. Yet the metaphor Oakeshott chose was not two-wheeled, but gastronomic. Like garlic in the hands of a cook, power must be wielded with discretion. Only its absence should be noted. Government appears, then, as the indispensable pepper; an aspect as vital to society, he says, as laughter is to happiness. Government cannot lead us to paradise, just as a joke cannot teach us the truths of the universe; and yet, the former saves us from the hell of civil war, while the latter saves us from taking ourselves too seriously. That was his calling: never to make too much of politics.

One mustn't make too much of politics, because one mustn't expect too much of mankind. On one occasion, one of his disciples asked him what he thought of mankind. Oakeshott remained silent for a moment, then said that he thought men were like cats: they took themselves too seriously. That was the worst vice of man, and the most hazardous vanity in politics.

---

[10] That's what Adam Gopnik calls him in a fine portrait of Oakeshott: "A Man without a Plan," *The New Yorker* (New York: October 21 and 28, 1996).

"Thomas Hobbes, the second son of an otherwise undistinguished vicar of Westport, near Malmesbury, was born in the spring of 1588." Thus begins Michael Oakeshott's brilliant introduction to the *Leviathan*, the work he defined as "the greatest, perhaps the sole, masterpiece of political philosophy written in the English language." Was Oakeshott exaggerating? No: Hobbes' monster isn't just an ingenious piece of philosophical perception. It is also a jewel of poetic intelligence. The *Leviathan,* Oakeshott writes, is "a myth, the transposition of an abstract argument into the world of the imagination."[11] Reason sheds light on even the most shocking fiction of the State.

Thomas Hobbes –that radical skeptic, that arrogant dogmatic– was the protagonist of Oakeshott's work. The Genius of Malmesbury allowed him to carve out a philosophical identity based not only on affinity, but contradiction as well. While preparing the introduction to Blackwell's edition of the *Leviathan*, the Covent gardener highlighted Hobbes' clarity, humor, imagination, ironic acidity, and polemic forcefulness. But he also pointed out the excesses of his sated intelligence. There is a systemic ambition in Hobbes that Oakeshott explicitly rejects: desiring all phenomena to fit together, creating a perfect artifact of ideas was, to him, a rationalist disorder. Hobbes fires out concepts; Oakeshott takes his ideas for a walk. Hobbes' sentences are not open to appeal; Oakeshott's notes are provisional. Hobbes defines, Oakeshott comments. To a large extent, Oakeshott's work is basically a lengthy critique of that *science* Hobbes wanted to found.

---

[11] "Introduction to the *Leviathan,*" in *Rationalism in Politics,* p. 222.

But his essays are also a dilated variation on the Hobbesian image of mankind. Human nature is the curse of politics; that is why political philosophers confront darkness. Oakeshott does not try to illuminate these shadows, or sublimate the sacrifices of power.

> Politics at any time are an unpleasing spectacle. The obscurity, the muddle, the excess, the compromise, the indelible appearance of dishonesty, the counterfeit piety, the moralism and the immorality, the corruption, the intrigue, the negligence, the meddlesomeness, the vanity, the self-deception, and finally the futility,
>
> Like an old horse in a pound,
>
> offend most of our rational and all our artistic susceptibilities.[12]

Scientists will try to seek out the ultimate logic of power, just as aesthetes will try to embellish the sovereign's face and feats; but all of them have forgotten that politics is an ugly stone, blasted by the sands of circumstance. It is in this gritty raw material of history, not on the smooth canvas of the geometricians, that we find the elements to *somehow and to a certain degree* fix the imperfections in public affairs. That is why the Statist is not a technician; rather, he's an artless artist.

> In political activity, then, men sail a boundless and a bottomless sea; there is neither harbour for shelter nor floor for anchorage, neither starting-place nor appointed destination. The enterprise is to keep afloat on an even keel; the sea is both friend and en-

---

[12] *The Politics of Faith...*, p. 46.

> emy; and the seamanship consists in using the resources of a traditional manner of behavior in order to make a friend of every hostile occasion.[13]

A philosophy of modesty that entails existentialism without melodrama. Political activity is a flotation device adrift on a sea of nonsense.

John Stuart Mill, convinced that all good comes from innovation, once said that conservatives, by virtue of their own existence, had formed the stupid party. Oakeshott intended to win some respect for the conservative temperament. He was conservative because he believed there was no need to declare war on circumstances; one must embrace them *affectionately*. Friendship is a bond of affection that cannot be corrupted by calculations of utility. "Friends are not concerned with what might be made of one another, but only with the enjoyment of one another; and the condition of this enjoyment is a ready acceptance of what is and the absence of any desire to change or to improve." Conservatism is, therefore, regard for circumstance. If Oakeshott embraced tradition, it is not because he blindly worshipped the past, but rather because he feared the consequences of syllogism. This man, who has been called the Burke of the 20th century, felt no sympathy whatsoever for external prescriptions of natural rights, or metaphysics of revealed truths. Unlike Burke, Oakeshott did not believe tradition was wise.

---

[13] "Political education," Oakeshott's inaugural conference at the London School of Economics, anthologized in *Reason and the Conduct of Political Life,* p. 60.

Burke had written that the snap judgments of individuals and groups tend to be mistaken, while those of the nation (a will that cuts across centuries) naturally encounter what is good. "The individual is foolish; the multitude, for the moment, is foolish, when they act without deliberation; but the species is wise, and, when the time is given to it, as a species, it almost always acts right."[14] For Oakeshott, the species is just as stupid as the individual or the masses. A silly remark repeated a thousand times does not magically turn into wisdom. Tradition is an incoherent soup of caprice and coincidence accumulated over the years.

> To be conservative, then, is to prefer the familiar to the unknown, to prefer the tried to the untried, fact to mystery, the actual to the possible, the limited to the unbounded, the near to the distant, the sufficient to the superabundant, the convenient to the perfect, present laughter to utopian bliss.[15]

Being conservative is a way of strolling through the world. It is an attitude or a mood, not a program. The conservative does not permit himself to be coerced by urgency and understands that there can be no unmitigated improvement. The notable thing about Oakeshott's conservatism is that it is completely devoid of dogma. The conservative disposition is not attached, in his case, to any concept of eternal good. Oakeshott's is, thus, a conservatism without ideology, a conservatism detached from right-wing

[14] Burke, *Speech on the Reform of the Representation of the Commons in Parliament,* in *Selected Works of Edmund Burke, Miscellaneous Writings* (Indianapolis, Indiana: Liberty Fund, 1999), p. 21.

[15] "On being conservative," *Reflections on Modern Politics,* p. 408.

preachiness. This is why sociologists of the new European left have sought solace in his pages. One of the first reviews of *Rationalism in Politics* appeared in the *New Left Review.* Colin Falck, the reviewer, suggested that Oakeshott's conservatism came very close to the fundamentals of socialist thinking. By emphasizing the concrete and the historical, his politics distinguished themselves from the empty framework of liberal values and the nostalgia of reactionaries. In short: it turns out that Oakeshott was practically a Marxist.[16] Anthony Giddens, father of the once fashionable Third Way –the program that endeavored to bring European leftist ideology up to speed in the late 20th century– appreciated Oakeshott's thinking as a prudent counterbalance to socialism. According to Giddens, the great message of his work is that everything is temporary, everything flows. History, as Burke pointed out, is a river that doesn't forget: nor does it long for its source. Oakeshott's conservatism lacks so much as a nostalgic grimace. He did not idealize the past; he did not falsify it by glorifying it –much less try to petrify it. What he did do was position himself in his own time in order to warn us of the technocrats' readiness to forget. Oakeshottian conservatism warns us against the fanaticism of political reason. Oakeshott learned this lesson from the author of those wise phrases about the French Revolution. The flour of politics is nothing more than time and place: pure circumstance. One must be conservative in a non-conservative fashion, Giddens concludes. Without a

[16] Colin Falck, "Romanticism in Politics," *New Left Review,* no. 18 (January-February, 1963).

conservative anchor, man lives as if he were a foreigner, floating above an Earth he'd like to remake, but never quite manages to touch or understand.[17] In other words: one must be conservative in an Oakeshottian fashion.

I am conservative in politics so that I can be radical about everything else, Oakeshott used to say. That is why *his* tradition is no remote garden to be revered; rather, it is an unavoidable circumstance. That which intends to raise itself up outside history seeks the aura of charisma, says the brilliant historian of ideas J.G.A. Pocock in an essay honoring Oakeshott.[18] Tradition is not a moral repository: it is the fountainhead of prudence. As long as we understand society to be a stream of actions incorporated over time, we will be kept safe from those saviors who believe not one drop of the past can touch them.

Oakeshott's conservatism is the child of his mistrust in humanity. His sole compass is doubt, or rather, suspicion. His is a "disturbed vision of the weakness and wickedness of mankind and the transitoriness of human achievement."[19] The founding fathers of this reflection are John Donne, the poet of fragility; Pascal, the mystic of grief; Hobbes, the philosopher of fear; and Montaigne. Above all, Montaigne. Understanding Oakeshott's po-

---

[17] Anthony Giddens, *Beyond Left and Right. The Future of Radical Politics* (Stanford, California: Stanford University Press, 1994).

[18] "Time, Institutions, and Action: An Essay on Traditions and Their Understanding," Preston King and B.C. Parekh, Eds., *Politics and Experience. Essays Presented to Professor Michael Oakeshott on the Occasion of his Retirement* (Cambridge: Cambridge University Press, 1968).

[19] From "The fortunes of scepticism," in *The Politics of Faith and the Politics of Scepticism*, p. 75.

litical skepticism presupposes delving into the thought of these geniuses. Donne, a poet of great complexity and emotional contradiction, described in *An anatomy of the world* the gloom of radical uncertainty:

And new philosophy calls all in doubt,
The element of fire is quite put out;
The sun is lost, and th'earth, and no man's wit
Can well direct him where to look for it.
And freely men confess that this world's spent,
When in the planets, and the firmament
They seek so many new; they see that this
Is crumbled out again to his atomies.
'Tis all in pieces, all coherence gone;
All just supply, and all relation:
...
This is the world's condition now, and now
She that should all parts to reunion bow,
She that had all magnetic force alone,
To draw, and fasten sundered parts in one;
....
She that was best, and first original
Of all fair copies; and the general
....
She, she is dead; she's dead: when thou knows't this,
Thou know'st how lame a cripple this world is.

Images of this wandering planet ("how lame a cripple this world is") overlap one another in Donne's poetry, from his love poems to his elegies.

> The heavens rejoice in motion, why should I
> Adjure my so much loved variety,
> And not with many youth and love divide?
> Pleasure is none, if not diversified:
> The sun that sitting in the chair of light
> Sheds flame into what ever else seems bright,
> Is not contented at one sign to inn,
> But ends his year and with a new begins.
> All things do willingly in change delight,
> The fruitful mother of our appetite.

Man, on the other hand, is a builder of ruins, a blind animal who kills in order to propagate his race.

> We seem ambitious, God's whole work to undo;
> Of nothing he made us, and we strive too,
> To bring ourselves to nothing back; and we
> Do what we can, to do't so soon as he.[20]

John Donne describes the core of our contradiction, the impossible fixation of our spirit: "Waters stink soon, if in one place they bide." It is the absurdity of permanence. Even that which is beautiful is fleeting. Therefore, variety is our lot in life. And science? An ignorance that denigrates us. The new medicine, he writes, is even more perniciously ingenious than syphilis.

Pascal's suffering is also present in Oakeshott's skepticism. Frightened by the "eternal silence of those infinite spaces," Pascal passionately shows us man gone astray,

---

[20] C.A. Patrides, Ed., *The Complete English Poems* (New York: Alfred A. Knopf, 1991).

the voids of his reason, the vanities of his science. Our surroundings are inevitably undecipherable. And any effort to solve the mysteries of existence borders on blasphemy. What Kolakowski calls Pascal's *sad religion* parts from the darkest anthropology: man is a lost animal, a grain of dust in the infinite universe, an abandoned creature who faces the future without hope, like a man condemned to death who witnesses his neighbor's execution each day. "Between us and heaven or hell there is only life, which is the frailest thing in the world," wrote this man, who lived every day of his life in pain. "We are fools to depend upon the society of our fellow-men. Wretched as we are, powerless as we are, they will not aid us; we shall die alone. We should therefore act as if we were alone..."[21] From where else should politics spring, if not despair?

Science, as mundane entertainment, is incapable of providing an answer to the drama of our existence. That's why Oakeshott finds in Pascal a brilliant exposé of the limitations of rationalism. The problem does not lie in his assessment of technical understanding, but rather his type of understanding. Reason cannot be excluded from human life, nor can man live on reason alone.

For Oakeshott, the ringleader in this line-up of skeptics is Montaigne, that joyful skeptic, that easygoing rambler. To him, uncertainty was no longer cause for distress. His lack of conviction brought a smile to his face. During his strolls, the fluctuation of the universe was no longer

---

[21] This essay cites paragraphs 206, 211 and 213 of Pascal's *Pensées*, in the Washington Square Press 1965 edition. Kolakowski's essay is *God Owes Us Nothing. Pascal's Sad Religion* (Chicago, Illinois: University of Chicago, 1996).

perceived as a nightmare, becoming instead a changing panorama of flavors and textures, of airs and climates.

Michel de Montaigne was born between 11 a.m. and noon on the last day of February, 1533. The beams in the ceiling of his library, like epigraphs that open the world of his mind, set the tone for his work: "It can be thus, and it cannot be thus." "I do not decide anything." "I understand nothing." "I examine." "No man has known or ever will know anything for certain." "Man is made out of clay." Among these pillars, Montaigne wrote man's self-portrait. I am the theme of my book, he warned his readers. And it's true: Montaigne speaks of his complaints and his tastes, his affections and his readings. But this subject –Montaigne– soon unfolds into the subject of man. Who is man? Which are the forms of his reason? What is the texture of his history? The answers to these questions sketch themselves out during his walks. At no point do they take on the symmetry of a system, or the decisiveness of a doctrine. They are essays. That is how you portray a place in ongoing flux: "The world is but a perennial see-saw. Everything in it – the land, the mountains of the Caucasus, the pyramids of Egypt –all waver with a common motion and their own Constancy itself is nothing but a more languid rocking to and fro."[22] If Montaigne cannot fix objects in the universe, it is because they themselves tremble, possessed by a natural intoxication of sorts.

And nothing is so changeable as man. In the essay on the inconstancy of our actions, man appears as an animal that adopts the colors of any place he finds himself in: a

[22] "On repenting," book III, p. 232. *The Essays: A Selection*, Ed. M.A. Screech (London: Penguin Classics, 1993).

creature that follows the changing fancy of his own appetites. Montaigne's self-portrait describes us all. "Every sort of contradiction can be found in me, depending upon some twist or attribute: timid, insolent; chaste, lecherous; talkative, taciturn; touch, sickly; clever, dull; brooding, affable; lying, truthful; learned, ignorant; generous, miserly and then prodigal – I can see something of all that in myself, depending on how I gyrate..." What is the proper suit to be worn by all men living in Montaigne's skin? What will be their true precept, their authentic design? The answer is clear: if he were to introduce a master rule, a capital principle, an order that envelops all men, Montaigne would end up asphyxiating them all. Definition is suicide, the jail of identity.

Montaigne did not idolize science: far from it. I know a hundred artisans who are happier than if they were university deans, he writes. The endeavors of the scientist do not bring him closer to happiness, or even to true knowledge. What is regarded a scientific hypothesis today will be crossed out tomorrow as ignorant fantasy. What is true from this window becomes false in that valley. The road to wisdom is experience. No science, no wisdom comprised of generalizations and abstractions can be capable of appreciating the universal law of diversity. Science tends to barricade itself from knowledge because it lacks the necessary imagination to combine realities and incorporate contradictory truths. The arrogance of believing our own thoughts is the worst sort of plague. The science books tend to clog up the pores of our skin with their pedantry. The world of scientific reason has made asses out of us, overburdened with books.

When I play with my cat, who's to say she isn't amusing herself with me? No certainty can be fixed in this sea of doubt. Out of these doubts –not out of nostalgia– Montaigne's conservatism was born. Skepticism erases any hope of finding the ideal architecture of society. Montaigne knew the fragility of man, society, power, law. The skeptic doesn't dream of a perfect world, nor does he throw himself into the pit of pessimism. He embraces what is there, recognizing always that it has been constituted by the radical fissure of our nature. It's no wonder, then, that the core of his conservative discourse can be found in the essay against vanity. "Nothing presses so hard upon a State as innovation: change only gives form to injustice and tyranny." But despite the severity of such verdicts, Montaigne does not intend to hamstring the State. What he rejects is the pretense of integrally changing politics, something he refers to later as "great mutations." If an element fails us, it must be fixed or changed; but any desire to re-pour the foundations of the public edifice is a depraved impulse. Evil is not always substituted by good: it tends to be substituted by another evil, an even worse one. Confronted by the arrest of revolutionaries, Montaigne defends a docile political will: "We do not go, we are driven; like things that float, now leisurely, then with violence, according to the gentleness or rapidity of the current." The sentence that best sums up this conservative disposition is found in Montaigne's essay on the art of conversation: "we must live amongst the living."

Like the Montaigne his father had taught him to admire, Oakeshott had no interest in drafting any philosophical treatises. His writings are simply, as he himself apprised, "footprints in the snow." His paragraphs walk, rather than run. Like Montaigne's exercises, in Oakeshott's writings, judgment is taken for a stroll. And this is the image he sustains not only of the game of philosophy, but of politics itself. Politics not as an argument, but as a conversation. Governance is a dialogue with circumstances, not an imposition.

> In a conversation the participants are not engaged in an inquiry or a debate; there is no 'truth' to be discovered, no proposition to be proved, no conclusion sought. They are not concerned to inform, to persuade, or to refute one another, and therefore the cogency of their utterances does not depend upon their all speaking in the same idiom; they may differ without disagreeing. Of course, a conversation may have passages of argument and a speaker is not forbidden to be demonstrative; but reasoning is neither sovereign nor alone, and the conversation itself does not compose an argument... Thoughts of different species take wing and play round one another, responding to each other's movements and provoking one another to fresh exertions. Nobody asks where they have come from or on what authority they are present; nobody cares what will become of them when they have played their part. There is no symposiarch or arbiter; not even a doorkeeper to examine credentials. Every entrant is taken at its face-value and everything is permitted which can get itself accepted into the flow of speculation. And voices which speak in conversation do not compose a hierarchy. Conversation is not an enterprise designed to yield an extrinsic profit, a contest where a winner gets a prize, nor is it an activity of exegesis: it is an unrehearsed intellectual adventure. it is with conversation as with

> gambling. Its significance lies neither in winning nor in losing, but in wagering. Properly speaking, it is impossible in the absence of a diversity of voices: in it different universes of discourse meet, acknowledge each other and enjoy an oblique relationship which neither requires nor forecasts their being assimilated to one another.[23]

In these lines we find both the profundity and the vacuum of Oakeshott's political theory. The revelation that government action is not demonstrative is a profound one. Governance is a test of action that must wait for a reply before formulating its next move. Politics, thus, is not a science or an art, it's a game.[24] But in this haphazard conversation, there is one thing that can never be given: an order. Voices are intermingled in a friendly fashion around English high tea at five in the afternoon. There is no hierarchy, no command, no final verdict. Gentlemen are entertained as they while away an agreeable afternoon. Words come and go. They turn the corner, change in tone, leap from one subject to the next, and arrive at nothing. Still, his aversion to political heroism may have gone too far. In Oakeshott's gathering, the teeth of force are never bared. Yet teeth, "armed guardians of the mouth," as Elias

---

[23] "The voice of poetry in the conversation of mankind," in *Rationalism*, p. 489.

[24] Parliamentary life, Oakeshott suggests in *The Politics of Faith*... isn't really that serious: it is a game in which friends appear as opponents, where there are disputes without hatred, conflicts without violence. The important thing in these rituals isn't the result, but rather the process. In this regard, Oakeshott summarizes the brilliant Dutch historian Johan Huizinga's reflections on *homo ludens*. "The very existence of play continually confirms the supra-logical nature of the human situation," Huizinga claims. "We play and we know that we play, so we must be more than merely rational begins, for play is irrational." Johan Huizinga, *Homo Ludens* (Boston: Beacon Press, 1970), pp. 3-4.

Canetti calls them, are the most notorious instruments of power. His would appear to be a toothless, powerless political philosophy. And power is what happens the moment the friendly chat has ended. One speaks while another is silenced; one commands while another obeys; one survives while another falls down dead. Like a sharp stinger, order cannot be argued against, altered, or appealed. Even in the sweetest of metaphors of power composed by Canetti, the contrast with the image of conversation is crystal clear. I am thinking here of his vignette about the orchestra director, a figure the great Bulgarian essayist sees as the most vivid expression of power:

> The conductor *stands*: ancient memories of what it meant when man first stood upright still play an important part in any representations of power. Then, he is the only person who stands. In front of him sits the orchestra and behind him the audience. He stands on a dais and can be seen both from in front and from behind. In front his movements act on the orchestra and behind on the audience. In giving his actual directions he uses only his hands, or his hands and a baton. Quite small movements are all he needs to wake this or that instrument to life or to silence it at will. He has the power of life and death over the voices of the instruments; one long silent will speak again at his command.[25]

Even in this musical scenario, in which director and musicians follow the same score, power perceivably marks a brusque division. The director stands alone in an elevated

---

[25] Elias Canetti, *Crowds and Power* (New York: Farrar, Straus and Giroux, 1984), p. 209.

position, all eyes on him. He causes them to speak or fall silent. In other words, the director does not converse: he directs. He hears the instruments, but his baton rules over them. In other words, Oakeshott discards that which is most characteristic of politics: power, passion, struggle, violence. Like Plato, Hanna Pitkin says, Oakeshott is so concerned over the threats of power and conflict that, instead of seeking a solution to problems they generate, he attempts to wipe them off the map once and for all.[26]

There's a word that appears over and over again on Oakeshott's tongue that no one would expect to find in a conservative's personal vocabulary. That word is *adventure*. History, the human condition, apprenticeship, life: four adventures, four encounters with the unexpected. It is a word conservatives tend to pronounce while lifting their eyebrows in a disapproving gesture. An adventurer is an irresponsible man who does not attend to his duties, a vagabond. To conservatives, adventure generally means forgetting life's commitments. But not *this* conservative. Adventure is his most precious word. Life adopts this shape of hazard and risk. Human life is essentially an adventure, he says in one of his essays on education. Traveling aimlessly, getting caught up in surprises, letting oneself be assailed by the unexpected; all of this forms part of the human condition: "Being human is a historic adventure."[27] History is an endless series of unfinished

---

[26] Hanna Fenichel Pitkin, "The Roots of Conservatism. Michael Oakeshott and the Denial of Politics," in *Dissent,* no. 4 (Fall 1973).

[27] "A Place of Learning," in *The Voice of Liberal Learning* (Indianapolis, Indiana: Liberty Fund, 1989), p. 16.

journeys: a variety of abandoned expeditions; an unending catalog of inconclusive explorations, the march of Fortune. Training for these galloping contingencies is not the equivalent of acquiring information. It is not about learning tips from a manual. It is about embracing the seduction of adventure.

History ventures. Life ventures. Itineraries are for trains, not men. Surprise, improvisation, risk, unexpected joys, the precipitation of disgrace. Discovering the world, discovering oneself. Oakeshott's fondness for the familiar is not the same as being devoted to routine. On the contrary, he flirts with risk. He repudiates any convention that pontificates: an audacious, sober move, one made out of intuition. It is said that in Margaret Thatcher's day, conservatives wished to honor Oakeshott with a title of knighthood. A week before this distinction was made official, something that made the Tories change their minds became public knowledge. The 70-year-old professor had been surprised by a police officer having sex with his wife on a beach. Suddenly, this sage man was no longer worthy of tribute. A right wing that had declared itself the solemn guardian of good manners was incapable of appreciating Michael Oakeshott's adventurous conservatism.

To confront ideological politics meant more to Oakeshott than taking a position on the limits of political understanding: it was a vital concept expressed quite clearly in the slim volume on horse racing he had coauthored with Guy Griffith, *A Guide to the Classics: Or how to pick the Derby winner.* After analyzing the characteristics of racehorses with great care, Oakeshott concluded that in reality, there is no guide to picking a winner at the races. His message to all those who wish to bet and win at the track is the same as the warning he extends to all those who are interested in wielding power: wisdom is a sense of smell, it cannot be reduced to how-to manuals. A true political genius is one who is drenched in a country's traditions and can respond with agility to different circumstances. Life itself is a game whose outcome no one knows. A judicious man accepts the limitations of his knowledge and knowingly bets on the risks every gamble implies. As one devoted admirer put it:

> The key to Oakeshott is to be found in that little book on the Derby. He rejoiced that life was a gamble. There was no device, ideology, method of reasoning, ruse, by which men could bet on a certainty and forecast how to turn fate to their advantage. He felt a faint contempt for those who want such certainty – even for those who think that by putting their trust in some economic theory they can shorten the odds. Why should they expect a political philosopher to predict which horse will win?[28]

Why, indeed?

[28] Noel Annan, *Our Age. English Intellectuals Between the World Wars. A Group Portrait* (New York: Random House, 1990), p. 400.

Bobbio And Goya's Dog

During one of Norberto Bobbio's final visits to Madrid, he asked to be taken to the Prado Museum. On his way out, he quipped: *Ma che saggio questo Goya: sapeva che l'uomo e cattivo*. How wise this Goya was: he knew that man is evil. He had just finished viewing the black paintings from the Deaf Man's Villa. Portrayals of oblivion, violence, despair. Darkness no longer as background, but as subject, *the* subject of Goya's painting. In *Fight with Clubs*, two men buried up to their knees beat each other with irons. They look like two giants bent on killing one another. One of them shows traces of blood on his face. The ending has already been given away: there is no escape; both of them will die. Bobbio must have noted Saturn's terrible stare as he bites down on the bleeding arm of his child; also the howling witches, the diabolical goats, the indigent masses. Perhaps he lingered before *The Dog*, Goya's finest portrayal of our condition, in which he shows the dog in all of us. We are engulfed in quicksand under a rusty sky. We look to the heavens, only to find no one is there. We are alone.

The wisdom Bobbio saw in Goya was one he shared: pessimism. The dark brushstrokes corroborated Bobbio's understanding of politics, his reading of history, his perception of mankind. In his Black Paintings, his vignettes on war, his landscapes decorated with thieves, the prints he composed about death, his caricatures of donkeys, and his mockery of priests and Inquisitors Goya binds humanity to its own flesh. In *The Disasters of War*, the painter outlines violence under no illusion of serving a noble cause.

For centuries, war has been a recurring aesthetic theme. For the most part, this art did serve a cause: by showing the crudity of war, artists have educated us for peace; by showing sacrifice, they have called us to combat; by depicting victory, they have inflamed our patriotic pride. Goya does not exploit this sentimentalism. He shows that the purpose of war is death, and that the death wish of others is what turns us into beasts –or rather, *reveals* that we are beasts. There is nothing noble, nothing heroic, nothing beautiful about war. The deaf painter from Fuendetodos knew whom to fear. As the man who drew a thousand monsters wrote in a letter: I'm not afraid of witches, or spirits, or the devil. The only creature that frightens me is man.[1]

Bobbio shared this fear. Man is a wolf to man, as Hobbes would say. An animal that kills for food, clothing, and even for entertainment, as the fuming reactionary Joseph de Maistre pointed out. Bobbio may have even coincided with Hegel regarding the image of history as a "huge slaughter-house." But unlike these spectators, Bobbio finds no hidden meaning in the butchery. In the sad story of mankind, Hobbes saw the mysterious hand of God; De Maistre, the brutal knee of Reason. Bobbio saw only the absurd. One of his final essays referred to a theme

[1] The letter is cited by Robert Hughes in *Goya* (New York: Alfred A. Knopf, 2003), p. 151.

that had accompanied him his entire life: Evil. This reflection by the aged Bobbio turned out to be a lucid, pessimistic allegation: in the broad economy of the universe, it is not the villain who suffers most, nor is it the hero who smiles at the end of the day. Whoever observes history without false hope will find the opposite is quite often true. Stalin died in bed; Anne Frank, in a gas chamber. History does not arrange events on the scales of justice. We all know better: justice does not exist.

Pessimism tends to be written off as a mood swing. But it isn't. Bobbio himself is tripped up by the same confusion when he writes, "pessimism isn't a philosophy, but a state of mind." And he tops it off by saying about himself: "I'm a pessimist in humor, not in concept." My impression is that Bobbio makes two mistakes. First, he disregards the philosophical dimension of pessimism; second, he misconstrues the root cause of his "state of mind." Pessimism is not the intellectual consequence of a depressive spirit, just as optimism is not the emanation of a festive temperament. John Stuart Mill, for example, was a man bedeviled by depression and yet, he was an incurable optimist. He believed in progress and the promise of the future. No matter how hard he searches, the pessimist fails to find that promise. Unlike those who dream of the best, he fears the appearance of the worst. Rather than a psychological disposition, pessimism entails a set of convictions regarding man and his place in history. According to Ambrose Bierce's dictionary, it is: "A philosophy forced upon the convictions of the observer by the disheartening prevalence of the optimist with his scarecrow hope and his unsightly smile."

Bobbio sees in himself a strong melancholy streak. But his pessimism is not so much a symptom of some psychological complaint as the product of his own intellectual convictions. In the first place, he knows that no matter how many centuries History accrues, man's skeleton remains the same. No matter where he stands, man is still a creature of machinations and madness, of games and wars. He can change his customs and beliefs; he can raise and tear down empires; he can improve the machines he manufactures. But man will continue to be the same beast Machiavelli described. In every age, the Florentine said, men are "ungrateful, fickle, false, cowardly, covetous."[2] These are not cultural vices or provincial diseases: they form part of our constitution, our cell structure. That is why the lessons of great thinkers are always contemporary. They have not been altered by the changing decor of history.

Like Cioran, Bobbio stands firm against any idolatry of Tomorrow. Progress is not the key to history. Skepticism is at the root of this conviction. We can never know everything. Those who know everything soon wish to kill everyone, as Alberto Camus once said. And what we do know, no matter how little it is, is not encouraging. Upon turning of the screw of doubt we find a simple belief: expect nothing from the future. His natural inclination, as Bobbio himself said, was "to always expect the worst."

George Steiner said that literary criticism should arise from a debt of love. It is this gratitude that drives those who write about the writing of others. The critic

---

[2] This is how Machiavelli puts it in Chapter XVII of *The Prince*.

is moved by a debt of love: after reading a novel, he becomes another person. The work has transformed him. After seeing a painting by Cézanne, Steiner writes, we see apples in a whole new way, as if we had never seen a real one. Steiner feels compelled to profess his admiration, because contemporary critics have confused this task with that of toppling statues. Biographers have become miners of vice and weakness. The industry of criticism is not unlike a scattergun of scandal. The great hero is exposed as a coward, the ingenious novelist becomes a plagiaristic wife beater, the architect admired by one and all turns out to be an alcoholic racist. Criticism used to be about turning illustrious men into saints. Today, it's the exact opposite: all men are pigs, starting with philosophers, artists, and other important figures.

The art of criticism, Steiner says, should be taken up as celebration, not censure. The critic shouldn't waste his time on anything unless it's worth the trouble. His gaze should be fixed only on masterpieces, lasting works of art. The publicists can see to all the mediocre novels that make their appearance on a weekly basis. Criticism is the fruit of admiration, and the critic, a mediator between the genius and his public. The critic appreciatively bears witness to the genius, then reveals him to the public by explaining and upholding him. But what light does this reflection shed on the nature of political criticism? Can we say that while the critic of literature analyzes a sonnet and the critic of politics, an act of empire, the seed is the same? From this perspective, the critic of power is also a grateful lover. A man who loves democracy, independence, and justice will write to uphold his passion, defending it against all threats: arbitrariness, submissiveness, despotism. Thus, the political critic runs the risk of becoming a not-so-secret admirer. That which is lifelong devotion in the literary critic becomes a blind spot in his political counterpart. The critical impulse in politics cannot arise from love. Tocqueville understood this better than anyone: his adhesion to political causes (democracy, for example) can be only a moderate bond, never a boundless passion.

Nor is political criticism born out of hatred, which is simply another form of idealization. If lovers see only beautiful traits in the object of their affections, then haters find only repugnant characteristics in the Other. Those who loathe power make no effort to comprehend its origins; they simply accuse it of being the root of all evil. Anarchism is therefore a critique so radical that it devours itself in the end. In its abomination of power, it ignores everything power has to give. From whence should the first breath of political criticism be drawn, then? Not from faith (neither that of the lovers nor the haters), but from suspicion. Political criticism is pricked by a thorn, an intuition, a misgiving. It is not the urge to render tribute or to express admiring gratitude that fans the flame. Political criticism is not congratulatory. Although certain things ought to be celebrated, the festivities must never drown out critical mistrust. Even the most delicious political apple has its worms. In politics, there are no perfect works to which we may dedicate ourselves wholeheartedly. Affairs of state have produced Napoleons, yet they have failed to give rise to a single Bach.

Criticism is born not out of certainty, but out of suspicion. The critic starts to write not because of what he knows, but rather because of what he is able to intuit. The critic is not a recorder of events; he is an unpleasant judge of merit. He is not interested in what's going on, but in the meaning of what's going on. Like any critic, the political critic tries to clear up the chaos of meaning that is the world. He discerns between the important and the trivial, the hazardous and the beneficial, the useful and the valuable, the fake and the real. And he does this while keeping one eye on the future always. Going back to our first impulse, the one that concerned Steiner in the case of literary criticism, the framework governing our gaze must be one of suspicion, not hope. The uncertainty that accompanies the future is not the image of a future garden, but the possibility of disaster. All criticism of power arises out of the suspicion of impending doom.

Such is the conviction of a critic like Bobbio, who was convinced that pessimism is an indispensable companion on any political journey:

> I am quite happy to leave the pleasure of being optimistic to fanatics, by which I mean those who long for catastrophe, and to the fatuous, by which I mean those who think that everything comes right in the end. Today pessimism is a civic duty, if you will allow me to use that impolitic term. It is a civic duty, because only radical and rational pessimism can induce some slight reaction in those who, on one side or the other, have shown themselves to be unaware that when reason slumbers, monsters are created.[3]

---

[3] *Norberto Bobbio, A Political Life*, Ed. Alberto Papuzzi (Cambridge, Oxford, and Malden, Massachusetts: Polity Press, 2002). pp. 126-127.

The sleep of reason produces monsters. Again, the wisdom of Goya.

From the time he took his first steps, Norberto Bobbio's life resembled that of a soft, split branch. On one hand were the comforts of family life; on the other, the qualms of conscience. He was born in Turin on October 18, 1909. His father was a prestigious surgeon. Two servants and a chauffer also resided in the home where he lived as a child. Yet somehow, comfort turned out to be rather uncomfortable. The contrast between the wellbeing he enjoyed and the want he saw all around imbued his character with a nonconformity that was not so much rabid as it was somber. From a very young age he experienced privilege as penitence. This Turinese boy used to go on long vacations in the countryside, accompanied by his family and friends from their social circle. It was there that he became aware of the blows dealt by injustice. "My friends and I," he related in his most successful book, "would arrive from the city and play with the farmers' children. Among *us* there was total harmony. We played without realizing how many rooms there were in our houses, or what shirts we wore. But an immense barrier separated us from *them*. We couldn't help but note the contrast between our homes and theirs; between our clothes and theirs; between our shoes and their bare feet." This disparity was by no means trivial. As an elderly Bobbio would recall many years later, upon returning to the countryside for summer vacations each year, they would learn that one of their playmates had died over the winter.

Under the roof of the Bobbio household, there was a palpable affinity toward fascism. Its patriotic discourse of order and prosperity must have been music to the ears of Dr. Luigi Bobbio. Norberto, his son, listened in silence to their celebration of Mussolini. Although he had started down a different path, he didn't dare confront his father. He attended meetings in anti-fascist circles without openly opposing his family's inclinations. He lived a double life: the law student at Turin University was officially enrolled in Fascist University Groups, but by night, he frequented meetings among the Resistance. In one pocket, the Fascist Party membership card; in the other, pamphlets from the Liberal Socialist movement. This personal contradiction would last nearly the entire decade of the 1930's. More than a youthful episode, this incoherence would evolve into a life marked by indecision, a capacity to harbor the incompatible.

While Norberto Bobbio was attending anti-fascist meetings, he swore loyalty to the regime to secure a post as a professor of legal philosophy. His oath didn't do him much good. In 1935, at the age of twenty-six, he was thrown in jail. The police had started a file on him because of his frequent encounters with "adversaries of the regime." Behind bars, the young professor followed his family's advice. He took up paper and pen to write *il Duce*, whom he addressed as His Excellency:

> I, Norberto Bobbio, son of Luigi, born in Turin in 1909, graduate in law and philosophy, am currently a teacher in philosophy of law at this university. I am a member of the Fascist National Party and the Fascist University Group since 1928, when I

> went to university. I became a member of the Youth Vanguard in 1927, when the first group of the Vanguard was set up at D'Azeglio Senior Secondary School as the result of an assignment entrusted to comrade Battieri of San Pietro and myself. Because of a childhood illness that left me with ankylosis in the left shoulder, I was rejected at the medical check-up for military service, and was unable to join the Militia. I grew up in a patriotic and fascist family (my father, consultant surgeon at the San Giovanni Hospital in this city, has been a member of the Fascist National Party since 1923, one of my two uncles on my father's side is a general in the Armoured Corps in Verona, and the other is a brigade general at the Military School). During my time at university, I took an active part in the life and work of the Turin Fascist University Group, organizing student magazines, single issues and student trips, to the extent that I was given the task of giving commemorative lectures on the March on Rome and the Victory to secondary-school students. Finally, in recent years, after having completed my degrees in law and philosophy, I have devoted myself entirely to studying philosophy of law and publishing the articles and papers that have earned me the qualification to teach at university level. The theoretical basis of these studies has helped me to consolidate my political opinions and deepen my fascist convictions.[4]

Norberto Bobbio also expressed his devotion for Mussolini, praying that, "with his elevated sense of justice," he would generously intercede on his behalf. Over half a century later, the letter of this young man would return to haunt to the memory of a much older Bobbio,

---

4 *Norbert Bobbio, A Political Life.* pp. 28-29.

one who had remained silent regarding these events. The newspaper *Panorama* published the entire text in 1992. Upon reading this degrading missive, the man who was by then considered to be the patron saint of liberal leftists felt ashamed. He admitted it was a dishonorable letter. Why did I fall prey to abjection? He asked himself. How is it possible that an honest professor, dedicated to his studies, could have written such a letter? And then, Bobbio ventured a response. This is no excuse, he warned. A dictatorship corrupts the spirit of men, which leads to hypocrisy, lies, and servility. And mine was a servile letter. In order to free yourself from the pitfalls of a dictatorship, you need both strength and valor: I had neither. Bobbio was, in effect, no hero.

Bobbio rhythmically uttered the syllables of his repentance. I-am-a-shamed. He was a man ashamed of his weakness, of having masqueraded as a fascist among fascists and as an anti-fascist among anti-fascists. But he didn't excoriate himself with his own whip. He responded to those who were in a rush to collect him as a hunting trophy with a question of Fabio Levi's. If in times of racial persecution, many Jews were induced to baptism in order to save themselves, then to whom should we attribute the responsibility of this act: the convert, or his persecutor?[5]

The ghost of this incongruence –or weakness– would haunt him his entire life, despite his admirers' best efforts to put him on a pedestal. Those attempting to turn him to marble failed to take into account that the hero, as Savater

---

[5] Norberto Bobbio, "La historia vista por los perseguidores," *Fractal*, no. 20.

said, is an adorable monster of sorts, a character deformed by the bulk of his qualities. This wasn't the case with Bobbio. His weakness dramatized his true militancy: the cause of his vacillation. It can even be said that his personal malleability was the source of his intellectual vigor. Determination, that virtue of gladiators, can be a perversion of intelligence. The task of men of culture, as he would say, is to sow doubt.

In the early 1940's, Bobbio got his feet wet in the puddle of politics. His ambitions were more intellectual than political; he intended to serve the cause of reconciliation between those two banners of modernity: liberalism and socialism. Bobbio therefore approached a group of Italian philosophers, lawyers, and historians who tried to embody a politics that would promote equality while at the same time, defending and broadening freedoms. Carlo Rosselli tossed the first seeds of this project into the earth with his *Liberal Socialism*, a defense of democratic socialism that broke away from Jacobin heritage. The only way socialism could renovate itself would be by becoming the heir of liberalism's ends and means: to seek the liberation of man, to watch over the forms of the constitutional state. It is necessary, Rosselli wrote, that "the Socialists [must] recognize that the democratic method and the liberal climate constitute a conquest so fundamental to modern civilization that they must be respected even, and above all, when a stable Socialist majority controls the government."[6] Liberalism and socialism were rendered as

---

[6] Norbert Bobbio, *Ideological Profile of 20th-century Italy* (Princeton, New Jersey: Princeton University Press, 1995), p. 149.

two branches of the same civilization. In the liberal socialist movement, Bobbio found a platform from which he could politically project not only his convictions, but also his hesitations. The idea was to lay the groundwork that would reconcile justice and liberty. The movement explicitly positioned itself in the middle. To the right was the liberalism of indifference, to the left, authoritarian collectivism. Liberal socialism wanted to open up a *third way*. Out of this search, the Action Party was born, the only one that would ever run Bobbio as a candidate. In 1946, the professor-cum-politician undertook the painful task of campaigning. But his foray into the electoral arena was a disaster. On Election Day, his party came in last. Well behind the Christian Democrats that emerged victorious; and a far cry as well from the Socialists, the Communists, and all the other medium- or small-sized parties that took part in the fray. An enormous failure. To tell the truth, the fiasco was rather predictable. As Bobbio recognized upon recalling the episode, the Action Party was a party of intellectuals –a squadron of "generals without an army," he called it– one that failed to connect to the interests of real society. Bobbio told himself: "Enough. My political life is over."

The Action Party was disbanded and Bobbio concentrated on academics as professor of legal philosophy at the University of Turin. In 1945, he traveled to London, invited by the British Council. In contrast with fascist Anglophobia, the democratic left in Italy admired the fatherland of constitutionalism, particularly the Labor Party. A vital parliament and democratically structured parties were what constituted the foundation of a strong, efficient government, one that didn't incur in the abuses of despotism. The antennae of the professor from Turin were attuned to the isle. They attentively captured all that was published there. By that I mean: all that had been published in past centuries and all that was being published at the time. Perry Anderson is right when he warns that Bobbio's liberalism is written in Italian with a British accent. Hobbes, Locke, Mill –the theoretician of the State, of the constitution, and of the individual– are present in all of his allegations and are, perhaps, the trinity behind his philosophy. Others would grab his attention, but in every paragraph that Bobbio published, the points of this trident can be seen: a defense of State order, a demand for limitations, and an emphasis on the citizen.

As department head, he concentrated on the world of norms at first. A student of philosophy and law, he naturally became a teacher of legal philosophy. As a professor, Bobbio was dedicated to studying the language of rules, the content of law, the bond that links one norm to the next. In essays that quickly won him notoriety, he explored the debate on the fundamentals of coercion, as well as the relationship between force and law. In each of these fields he made valuable contributions. I will highlight only two themes here: first, his construction of critical positivism. For Bobbio, Law is a mandate of the State, not of Nature. Laws are not inscribed from heaven. They are not imprinted on some curve of our genetic code, nor is there a rule governing all men that is applicable during the entire course of History. Law, as Hobbes had perceived, emerges from the throat of the sovereign. There is no other law but that which is imposed by the State. The murals that throughout history have been painted by theologians and moralists to describe a universal, eternal code of rules are fantastical sketches. However, Bobbio doesn't deny that the moral content of Law can be evaluated.[7] Law could and should be subject to moral criticism, even when we cannot find an objective yardstick with which to measure morality.

But then, what's inside? What is the content of Law? Bobbio's blunt reply: force. Domesticated, but force nonetheless. "Law is the rule of force." It isn't advice, or a kind invitation: it is the administration of punishment. For legal norms to exist, they must activate the jaws of power. Hobbes put it superbly in his *A Dialogue between a Philosopher and a Student of the Common Laws of England*: "It is not Wisdom, but Authority that makes a Law... because none can make a Law but he that hath the Legislative Power."[8]

Underneath Bobbio's formula, Weber's realism and Kelsen's judicial positivism can be discerned. But primarily, we see there the white beard of Hobbes –the philosopher from Malmesbury, the author he most admired. Not for his dry understanding of State machinery alone, but for the implicit image it leaves behind on the void of legality. The State and its flip side, Law, may be threatening condensations of force, but their absence is a leap into the void. In the late 1970's, when Italy suffered the violence of extremism, Bobbio raised his voice in defense of an in-

[7] On this point, consult the study by Alfonso Ruiz Miguel, *Política, historia y derecho en Norberto Bobbio* (Mexico: Fontamara, 1994).

[8] (Chicago, Illinois: The University of Chicago Press, 1971), p. 3.

creasingly unpopular character: the State. The Leviathan takes on the shape of a monster, but it is the only creature that can win us peace, free us from fear, and make enough room for liberty. Unlike those who, out of vengeful anarchism or anti-political liberalism, chanted slogans against the fearsome State, Bobbio sided with it. Hobbes' heir wouldn't have it any other way.

It is only natural for revolutionaries to cloak their violence with arguments of retribution. Armed insurrection appears as the only viable response to State-backed violence. If the former violence (that of jail) is unjustifiable, then the latter (that of the bomb) becomes justifiable. The first difficulty lies in that according to any struggle, unjustified violence –that is to say, original violence– always comes from the other side: "He started it." The transposition of this argument to political discourse is no innocent, childish alibi. On the contrary, Bobbio says, the intellectuals who use this language to justify illegality are encouraging politically senseless and morally condemnable violence.

No one questions the fact that the State is an instrument of repression. All States are. But not all States are equal, as Lenin would have it. The subject of "original" violence is irrelevant. What matters is its institutional structure. The fundamental difference between violence of the State and that of its rivals is the nature of the State's institutionalization. Those who invoke Lenin to justify rebellion should read Locke, another revolutionary. The democratic pact domesticates force under the empire of rules. Rules are defended not in order to protect the palace, but rather to safeguard every person's home.

Bobbio was simply defending democracy. His statism had two targets. On one hand, the ideologues of redemptive violence who were throwing gasoline onto the flames; on the other, those who backed brute force. There is no greater test for a democratic regime, Bobbio maintained, than having to confront a war declared on it by some of its own members. In light of such a declaration, pluralism can turn only to the stone tablets of the Law.[9]

In 1959, while traveling through China, Franco Fortini, a travel companion, painted an eloquent portrait of the professor:

> He must be between forty and fifty years old. His entire person exudes not so much intellectual force as a kind of deep-rooted education and a loyalty to parents and grandparents. The energy behind his convictions has, in his case, the sole weakness of expressing itself for precisely what it is: namely energy. You feel that he is well aware of the virtues of order, tenacity, sober thinking and intellectual honesty. Such would perhaps have been accompanied by a kind of didactic intensity, if it were not offset every now and then by a smile which is both embarrassed and ironic. It is ironic, every time his speech indulges in a superfluous adjective or a tone that is just slightly more passionate than usual. It is embarrassment or even timidity when it suggests a hint of worldliness or nonchalance. It is clear that as a boy he must have been diligent and clever, and must have despised all forms of sentimental frailty.[10]

---

[9] *Ideologie e il potere in crisi* (Florence, Italy: 1981).
[10] *A Political Life*, pp. 85-86.

Fortuni captured Bobbio's internal motor: his *pedagogical passion*. Upon turning ninety, while his followers were competing for praise, he claimed that the title of "professor" was the only one he deserved. Someone asked him if he preferred to be considered a philosopher, an intellectual, or a politician. All three hats suited him well. This native of Turin had drafted an impressive library of legal and political philosophy; he was an authority on public debate; he had founded a misbegotten party and at the time, had been appointed Senator for life. But Bobbio the philosopher, the politician, the intellectual, emphasized his duty to the classroom. I am a professor, because a professor is not a thinker but rather, a man who transmits the thoughts of others. Bobbio's answer was not a show of false humility: the whisper of chalk gliding across the blackboard can be heard in everything he did. In his early incursions into politics and his vacillations as an old legislator, in his public polemics and his manuals, there is the same passion to communicate what he knows, the excitement of leading his readers towards an encounter with the grand old texts. As a teacher he used to say that before talking, before making a decision, one needs to think; and in order to think, one needs to take the time to learn. There are no shortcuts.

In the early 1970's, Norberto Bobbio left the School of Law and joined the recently founded Faculty of Political Sciences. From then on, he headed the department of political philosophy. Bobbio's approach to the subject matter was historical. He believed that, in order to analyze any political enigma, the most rewarding method was to go on an excursion through the history of Western thought. After the tour, concepts would be cleared of all ambiguities of common usage, allowing us to calibrate conflicting reasoning. A classic, Italo Calvino has written, is a text that never finishes saying what it has to say. It is also a text that provides the backdrop to our own perspective. Once we have read Machiavelli, we can never open our eyes the same way again.

At one point, Bobbio described himself as a "pedantic reader of the classics." He was clearly an obsessive reader of great political thinkers. He read and reread Machiavelli and Rousseau; Mill and Marx; Gramsci, Weber, and Kelsen. And above all, Thomas Hobbes. Always Hobbes. The adjective "pedantic" is, however, out of line. There is no pedantry whatsoever in Bobbio's reading of the classics. At no time do the outlines drawn on his chalkboard employ the jargon of doctoralism, nor do they fall prey to the minute details of erudition. Bobbio's prose advances with open, easy strides. He identified fundamental ideas, extracting their pulp in order to reconstruct the logic of their argumentation. Thus, he connected concepts to theories, revealing the contemporary nature of old reflections. He knew reading the ancients was an intelligent way to take part in the present. When the Spanish newspaper *El País* requested an article to commemorate an anniversary of Thomas Hobbes' birth, the professor answered swiftly. Of course: I'll write you an article on the Middle East. And he was right. Hobbes was there.

Bobbio's style inspired a school of thought in Turin. Indeed, revisiting the classics allows one to explore recurring issues in politics. Michelangelo Bovero, Bobbio's successor as chair of Political Philosophy, has accurately employed this method to analyze the dangers of contemporary democracy by evoking Polybius and his theory on mixed government. The Roman historian accepted that simple forms of government can be, as Aristotle sustained, virtuous modes of politics; however, they proved to be unstable. Monarchy would degenerate into tyranny; aristocracy –the government of the wisest– would be corrupted as oligarchy –the government of the privileged– and the Republic would devolve into demagogic chaos. The solution, he believed, was a blend of pure forms of government that would create a structure of checks and balances, thus ensuring permanence. But what Polybius failed to consider was that this mixture could very well end up using only the corrupt aspects of these forms of government. The combination of tyranny, demagoguery and oligarchy is what Bovero calls *kakistocracy*: bad government, a Republic of the worst components. Of course, Polybius' disciple wasn't toying with the theoretical possibilities his model entailed. He was invoking the Roman historian in order to describe the democratic degeneration provoked by Silvio Berlusconi's rise to power. The Italian kakistocracy is a global warning: a government that combines the despotic power of a charismatic leader, the privilege of the potentates, and media manipulation of the masses.

Bobbio's writing (essays, speeches, books, articles, conferences, and transcriptions of courses) inspired his student and translator José Fernández Santillán to say that his work has all the complexity of a labyrinth. The image is none too convincing. A labyrinth is an intricate structure of streets and crossroads that is very difficult to escape from. And we are never lost inside Bobbio's writing; on the contrary, whoever enters one of Bobbio's texts strolls across an open, sunny field. The image that best represents his work as a whole is the map, another of Borges' favored metaphors. Because Bobbio's chalkboard is just that: a broad map of politics. Among the many planes drawn by Bobbio we can find his aspiration of order, his tendency to offer us a coherent panorama of power –or rather, of how to think about power– while allowing us to pin down our position. Bobbio inscribes the location of ideas, he finds the outskirts and measures the distances. He is a cartographer who graphically represents the territory of Western political reflection. He does not find the isles of exception very interesting. He prefers the continents of great intellectual traditions: the natural preserve of Aristotle, the kingdom of Machiavelli and his disciples, the valley of Contractarianists, the great Marxist enclave. Bobbio was interested in the classics, not the oddities.

Not everything fits, of course, on the Turin chessboard. To make a map is to make a choice: some elements are enlarged, others are colored in, certain characteristics are eliminated. Every map is a reasoned caricature of sorts. Unlike the scientists from Borges' story, Bobbio was not drawing a map so detailed that it turned out to be the perfect reproduction of the territory it described: "a map of the Empire the same size as the Empire that coincided with it point by point." Bobbio's map is a plane that seeks the essential, one that simplifies and emphasizes. Naturally, it also excludes. The first element to be banished is time. The classics Bobbio refers to inhabit a world without years, a space devoid of circumstances.

Classical works contain a timeless wisdom. That is why they form part of the canon. Indeed, the sole context of classics consists of other classics.

Once History has been expelled from the blackboard, we can observe the staging of debates that have lasted for centuries. But this approach also has its risks. When we concentrate on the gallery of immortals and discard the extenuating circumstances of their work, we too easily ignore the vocabulary the author used to express and frame our perception of the dead. "Whoever is familiar with texts on political theory knows that for centuries, they have redefined certain fundamental themes; always the same ones." It is possible. Good government, modes of change, loyalty and disobedience, the origin of leadership: all have been, in effect, recurring themes. But when we try and analyze the answers given to these questions throughout history, we run the risk of turning the classics into marionettes. We take a medieval author, extract a passage in which he refers to the different functions of government, and make him appear to be a visionary, a forerunner of the balance of power theory. This is a vice, one that Quentin Skinner has intelligently denounced.[11] When the historian attempts to reconstruct the history of political ideas by sanctifying a club of immortals, he tends to assume that his classics respond to each of the fundamental problems, and that every philosopher has an answer (albeit an underdeveloped one) to the eternal questions. A single paragraph can turn Machiavelli into a

[11] Quentin Skinner, "Meaning and Understanding in the History of Ideas," in *Visions of Politics, Volume I: Regarding Method* (Cambridge: Cambridge University Press, 2002).

theoretician of multiculturalism, or Montesquieu into the realist who predicted swift response to terrorist threats.

The second element expelled by the Bobbian outlook is the Author. Any reader of manuals could put together the pieces of the artifact invented by Hobbes: his idea of Man, his vignettes on the natural condition, or the judicial characteristics of the contract, the form of the State, the civil condition. But he would learn nothing about the individual who wrote these paragraphs. Nothing of the fear he described as his twin. Nothing of the wasp's nest in which he lived. A great admirer of Hobbes and a careful reader of the *Leviathan*, the treatise on the citizen, the essay on natural law, the Behemoth, and other, lesser texts; Bobbio rules out in his analysis anything that was never put on paper. Hobbes' skull, for example, which according to one of his biographers was shaped like a hammer. The exclusion of these traits is deliberate: Bobbio's safari goes out in search of concepts, pushing aside any historic or biographical references. This was one cartographer who believed that any reference to circumstance was an "extravagance of historicism."[12]

I do not mean to scorn Bobbio's didacticism. There are not many more lucid guides available for an expedition through the polemics of power. Therein, we find a map

---

[12] This warning from Bobbio is clear: "In studying authors from the past, I've never been especially attracted by the mirage of the so-called historical framework, which elevates sources to precedents and events to conditions, becoming so diluted at times in the details that it loses sight of the big picture: I have dedicated myself, on the other hand, with particular interest to the explanation of fundamental themes, the clarification of concepts, the analysis of arguments, and the reconstruction of the system." *From Hobbes to Marx*, quoted in Alfonso Ruiz Miguel's prologue to *Estudios de historia de la filosofía* (Madrid: Editorial Debate, 1985).

of bifurcations: political efficiency and moral conscience, law and repression, machine and organism, stability and change, obedience and rebellion, public square and palace, public and private, legality and legitimacy, civil society and the State. Bobbio is a master of classification; his method is a powerful detergent of political language. And that, in and of itself, is invaluable during an era of muddy vocabulary. It should come as no surprise that one of his most important works was an unabridged political dictionary, and that the rest of his books are a stubborn invitation to put words in order. The clarity Bobbio's writing boasts is not always accompanied by profundity. A great deal of his bibliography consists of academic manuals: pedagogical instruments that do not offer new insights, subtle observations, or sharp discoveries that examine the History of Ideas. His compendium *From Hobbes to Marx*, or his *General Theory of Politics* are just that: classroom notes transformed into books. That is his scope. When Perry Anderson, the Marxist historian who studied his writing in depth, said Norberto Bobbio wasn't actually an original philosopher of great stature, he was telling the truth.

Bobbio dedicated himself to the task of cleaning up political language. That was the mission of his philosophy: to build concepts, transforming the soap bubbles issued from the demagogue's mouth into bricks of understanding. Bobbio was horrified by vagueness and muddled thinking.[13] He explored the hallways of history

[13] When he speaks of Julien Benda in these terms, he is actually speaking of himself and "...his passion for net definitions, combined with his terror of vagueness and muddled ideas, unable to integrate well-defined relationships with other ideas." *La*

in order to pin down the meaning of ideas. And there was no word Bobbio was more determined to disinfect than *democracy*. No combination of syllables was capable of producing as much salivation in the 20th century as this blend of Greek voices. But what is democracy? What has it been? What can it become?

His first approach to this subject was an essay Bobbio published a few months after Stalin's death. His incentive was the famous Khrushchev report denouncing the abuses of the previous era. Its title was typically Bobbian: "Democracy and dictatorship." The article called upon socialists to walk unaided by the crutches of Marx. Whenever we interrogate it on major political issues, Marxism remains silent. It has no answer. It is, in fact, a gigantic political loophole. Marx was concerned with other problems. Accordingly, the most urgent task of the left was to look to the architects of liberal institutions. The response from the mandarins wasn't long in coming. They accused him of being a reactionary, a traitor, a member of the bourgeoisie who intended to sink the ship of History and block the triumphant march of the working class.

Twenty years later, in the mid-1970's, Bobbio revisited these themes. In the Socialist Party magazine, he published essays about the absence of a Marxist political theory, and the absence of a Marxist alternative to representative democracy. The brief paragraphs that Marx dedicated to the French revolutionary experience weren't enough to form a notion of the State, or a consistent argu-

---

duda y la elección. Intelectuales y poder en la sociedad contemporánea (Barcelona: Paidós, 1998), p. 31.

ment regarding the form government should take. While Marxism is a critique of the political modes of capitalism, it does not take itself seriously as an alternative. There is no political theory because Marxism and, above all, Leninism dealt only with the conquest of power, neglecting the problems involved in wielding it. Marxism cannot conceal the fact that it was under the spell of an anarchist fantasy. After all, the State was destined to die out and be buried on the "trash heap of history."

Gaetano Della Volpe, a disciple of Mondolfo and of Togliatti, the leader of the Communist Party himself, responded. He saw Bobbio's invitation as a betrayal of Marx, an abandonment of Socialist thought, a rushing into the arms of Benjamin Constant –that engineer of enemy institutions. While Bobbio was reading the apostles of the bourgeoisie, the Communists were taking refuge in the mausoleums of Marx and Rousseau. Bobbio responded to the attacks with equanimity. He unraveled the threads of their arguments with great elegance and persuasive power, asking Della Volpe to distrust the "fiery progressiveness" that, amid fraternal slogans, led to single party dictatorship.

During the polemical clash, Bobbio stood his ground. He ducked Della Volpe's disqualifications gracefully; he heard out his arguments and debated them with great agility. He based his reasoning on the classics, spicing up his allegations with irony while never once looking down on his critics. He heard them out. He responded. During these interventions, Bobbio gently wove one of the most solid declarations ever in favor of democracy. His was, in effect, a democratic defense of democracy, a line of reasoning born within the forum of public discussion.

In direct confrontation with Marxist quoters, Bobbio reinforced his understanding of democracy. The democratic regime is described as a procedure that opens its doors to collective participation. It is a method, not a result. The main source of this procedural vision was the author who had wielded such a heavy influence over his legal writing: Hans Kelsen. The Austrian jurist understood democracy as a political regime under which citizens, either directly or indirectly, wrote the rules. Democracy is not a regime that expresses truth or justice: it is a political system where individuals participate in the formation of norms by electing those who dictate them. Kelsen also underlined the importance of competitive institutions, particularly political parties, and respect for minority rights. Without parties (the plural is essential here) there is no democracy. Nor can it exist without providing refuge for minorities.[14] Schumpeter would later reinforce this vision. Democracy is not, as the Rousseaunians would have it, the kingdom of the General Will; nor is it the conquest of public happiness. It is a modest, competitive procedure. As the Austrian economist sustained, it is a method where those in charge of decision-making come into power through electoral competition.[15]

Those were the ingredients for baking the cake: rules, competition, and rights. Democracy was tied to the empire of rules and tolerance. "What is democracy but a set of rules (the so-called rules of the game) to resolve conflicts without bloodshed?" Bobbio asks, paraphrasing

[14] *Essence and Value of Democracy.*

[15] *Capitalism, Socialism, and Democracy* (New York: Harper and Row, 1975).

Popper.[16] The Italian emphasized four fundamental principles of the democratic game: universal suffrage, majority rule, individual freedoms, and minority rights. Democracy was a procedure, not a substance; an ideal that should be wholeheartedly embraced by the left, because this was the only known space in which free, autonomous beings could coexist. Where a trail could be blazed by the collective will without crushing the voice of discrepancy. The theoretical void of Marxist politics would be unabashedly filled with liberalism. Those aware of the destructive capacity of power know that liberal institutions and practices are not the walls of a capitalist prison, but rather the columns of individual autonomy.

Thus Bobbio helped inject a liberal vaccine into a sizeable portion of the left. He did so from within, rejecting the dogmatism of the era. Democracy, which continued to be caricaturized within the Communist Party as a palace of deceit, or the tyranny of the triumphant bourgeoisie, was defined by Bobbio as a prerequisite for civilization. The task of the left was, in effect, to reconcile itself with liberalism while recognizing the value of democratic mechanisms. The contemporary left had to go back to being what it once was: liberal. While many argued about the objective conditions of revolutionary uprising and continued to dream of a direct assault on power, Bobbio defended such boring practices as suffrage, or constructs as unappealing as political parties. His allegations were not the campaign of an enthusiast; they were the persuasion of a disenchanted man. Perhaps liberal democracy

[16] *El futuro de la democracia* (Mexico: Fondo de Cultura Económica, 1996), p. 136.

won't assure a more humane exercise of power, only that the power will be less brutal. A small, but at the same time, enormous difference. For the same reason, whoever knows how to defend democracy also knows not to ask too much of it: "the only way to save democracy is by taking it as it is, in the spirit of realism, without giving or receiving false hopes."[17]

That is why any democrat must be, like Tocqueville, a critic of democracy. And Bobbio was a most energetic one. In one of his most popular essays, he presents democracy as a deception. Democracy is determined to promise what it can't deliver. Hence, what he calls the "unfulfilled promises of democracy." Democracy offered power to the people, it assured us cliques would be dismantled, it promised to spread until all social realms were covered, it swore to eliminate secrecy and cultivate virtue. None of this has happened. Actual democracy is riddled with flaws. The lobbyists and corporations impose their interests and secrecy shrouds the decision-making process, while the bureaucratic machinery continues to operate farther and farther away from the public eye. The citizen, shut off in his own world, can hardly be bothered by the spectacle. And yet, democracy continues to be a defensible ideal. Despite all its miseries, democracy deserves support more for the misery of its alternatives than on its own merit. Bobbio backs Churchill's expression: the only thing that saves democracy is the fact that other forms of government are much worse. All political decisions come down to choices between lesser evils.

---

[17] Bobbio says this in his review of Giovanni Sartori's *The Theory of Democracy Revisited*: "La democracia realista de Giovanni Sartori," *Nexos* (Mexico: February 1990).

The importance of Bobbio's argument lies, above all, in the territory from which it sprang. The democratic conceptualization he constructs is not quite original. Popper, Kelsen, Schumpeter had already assembled the procedural model. The important thing is that Bobbio speaks from the realm of the left. From there, he polemicizes with socialist intellectuals and spokespersons of the Communist Party. The title itself of the book containing his contributions to the debate is clearly a jibe: *Which Socialism?* This is the title of his thoughts on... democracy. Actually, the compilation is not a meditation on desirable socialism or the possible kinds of socialism, as the book jacket claims. It is a powerful defense of the democratic regime, its rules and values. It is also a warning about the difficulties and threats of pluralism. But the socialism on the cover is hidden among the pages. The word makes a timid appearance in the final paragraphs of the book and is painted in vague terms. Clearly, Bobbio wanted to address the socialists. He wanted to debate the left from its own territory and therefore duly employed its language and treated its idols with caution.

Bobbio's critique of Marxism in these early political essays is, quite frankly, feeble. Seen with the benefit of hindsight, one cannot help but notice the way in which Bobbio avoids confrontation with the marrow of historic materialism in order to take on easier targets. He hurls himself against Marxist fanaticism, but takes care not to criticize the logic of Marxism. He attacks the readers of Marx, not Marx himself; he criticizes what Marx doesn't say, rather than cast judgment on what he does say. He censures the absence of a Marxist political theory. He does not reproach

Marxists for who they are, but rather for being *exclusively* Marxist. Bobbio treats Marxism sentimentally. On one occasion, he spoke of Marxist philosophy as a moral, an ethical window that allowed us to see the drama of history from the side of the oppressed.[18] But Marxism is no Dickensian Christmas tale. Its fundamental pretension is philosophical –and not just any philosophy: that of the final liberation of man. Here then is a notion that Bobbio, who was a reader of Popper, dares not call by name. In his moment of greatest lucidity, his softness betrays him once more. As in his youth, when he took on the appearance of a fascist among fascists and a liberal among liberals, he was now representing himself as a kind of Marxist (heterodox, of course) among Marxists. But he was no such thing.

Rhetorical concessions can be effective. Outright criticism of Marxism would have made those he had chosen as interlocutors turn a deaf ear. But the strategy also trips him up on unsustainable absurdities. In defense of reformism, Bobbio writes: "If it is justifiable to speak of a reformist Marxism, Leninism and Reformism are two incompatible terms; to speak of Reformist Leninism would be to speak of a square circle." Then he crowns his political absolution of Marxism by separating it from its mistaken disciples. Whoever "thinks that Leninism is the natural consequence of Marxism –on a practical level, not just a

---

[18] In response to Palmiro Togliatti, Secretary of the Italian Communist Party, he wrote: "I am convinced that if we hadn't learned from Marxism to see history from the point of view of the oppressed, gaining a new and immense perspective in the human world, we wouldn't have been able to save ourselves." Here the jibe is even greater: Marxism as revelation, as the path to salvation. The quote is reprinted by Alfonso Ruiz Miguel in *Política, historia y derecho en Norberto Bobbio* (Mexico: Fontamara, 1994), p. 29.

theoretical one– is totally outside the logic and practice of Reformism." Can one, in effect, speak of a *reformist* Marx? No. Taking the Revolution out of Marx is like depriving Christians of heaven.

Bobbio had read Karl Popper's *The Open Society and Its Enemies* and, a year after it appeared in English, published a review praising the book. However, in his disputes with the left, he does not invoke the name of the man who exposed the totalitarian root of Marxist thinking. Invoking Popper would have crossed the line by setting up camp in right-wing territory. While Bobbio was publishing his arguments on democracy and at the same time avoiding confrontational questioning, Leszek Kolakowski was asking himself about the connection between Marxism and Stalinism.[19] The Polish philosopher maintained that Marxism contained the seed of totalitarian horror. The dream of liberated humanity implied the elimination of machinery instituted by the bourgeoisie. A reconciled society would need no laws, or State, or representative democracy, or individual freedoms. All these devices were seen as an expression of a market-dominated society. The political problem of Marxism isn't simply, as Bobbio would have us believe, its silences. One inevitably finds a totalitarian carapace in its structure.

Bobbio celebrated the fall of the Berlin Wall in his own way: with a warning. The demolition of the Wall blow by blow with hammers was a defeat of the bad left,

[19] "Marxist Roots of Stalinism," in Robert C. Tucker, *Stalinism. Essays in Historical Interpretation* (New York: Norton, 1977). Bobbio's book was published a year earlier in Italy.

and a reward for the good left. The repressive, despotic left had become so much rubble, martial symbols of the proletariat fatherland on sale to tourists. The project of fraternity ended up creating an oppressive, miserable jail. History and its surprises had proved Bobbio right. The program of the victorious dissidents was precisely what the Italian had asked of the left thirty years earlier: democratic liberties, protection from arbitrariness, freedom of the press, the right to assembly, freedom of association. But Bobbio was by no means dancing on the grave of totalitarian communism. The liberal space it gave way to couldn't be the end of the road. The democratic State that Bobbio always defended was as necessary as it was lacking. In a world of atrocious injustices, one cannot believe that the radical problems of coexistence will simply disappear thanks to a few formalities. Could triumphant democracies efficiently address the problem of inequality, or would they be trapped by procedural digressions? That would be his main challenge. Given the failure of communism, Bobbio renewed his faith in the left. He therefore set about specifying its nature.

We'd understand the world very differently if, instead of having two hands, two eyes, and a pair of legs, we were made another way. The body compels us to order the universe in pairs: day and night; cold and heat; up and down; yes and no. Surely the eight tentacles and single eye of the octopus register the marine world very differently than the view from our binary anatomy. French novelist Michel Tournier wrote a beautiful book about the couplings on which our worldview rests. Our minds work in pairs. Every body has a counterpart that is just as strong. Man and woman; laughter and tears; bull and horse; animal and vegetable; memory and custom; poetry and prose; god and the devil. Ideas, apparently, do not stand alone; they are linked to our understanding along with their opposites. He who has never tasted salt cannot know the flavor of sugar.[20]

Bobbio proceeds as follows: as a portrayer of political thought he outlines concepts, always keeping the silhouette of their shadows in mind. And there is no more relevant beacon of political action in the world than one that allows us to distinguish right from left. What does it mean to be "right wing" in the ideological theater? Who is a leftist? In common usage, one might say that the right wing implies preservation, a love for tradition that must be upheld despite the complainers who want to change everything. Whereas the left wing is a denunciation of the status quo, a rebellion against custom. Those on the right see the future as a threat, while those on the left intend to emancipate us from the chains of history. The former bow to the imperfections of our natural condition; the latter denounce the injustices of our circumstance. The sin of the right is cynicism; the sin of the left is naïveté. A right-winger, as Ambrose Bierce noted in his devilish dictionary, is a politician enamored of existing evils. He can be distinguished thus from the left-winger, who wants to replace them with new ones.

Some of those born in revolutionary times chose to do away with these distinctions. This particular compass, they said, is obsolete: two names that designate empty

[20] Michel Tournier, *The Mirror of Ideas* (Lincoln, Nebraska: University of Nebraska Press, 1998).

drawers, banners that no longer summon the combatants of contemporary politics. For Bobbio, the distinction continues to be as valid as it was on the day the seating arrangement was established at the French National Assembly. Then as now, left and right express the need for a sense of belonging, a primordial antagonism to divide the battlefield. This distinction, Bobbio would insist, not only continues to thrive in everyday language, but also in the reasoning behind it.

The gap between left and right is established by attitudes toward equality. This is Bobbio's argument. The left is essentially egalitarian. This is not because it intends to make humanity uniform or because it fails to recognize the existence and even the value of certain inequalities, but rather because it maintains that political action can and should make an effort to reduce disparities in the distribution of wealth and power. The right, on the other hand, believes that the project of equality is impossible or undesirable. From the left, it can be understood that men are, in many aspects, unequal. Actually, men among themselves are as equal as they are unequal. The important thing is that, from the left, one mostly appreciates the similarities, seeking above all to eliminate the abysses of inequality. The left seeks to smooth out our differences; the right intends to reinforce them.

> We can then correctly define as egalitarians those who, while not ignoring the fact that people are both equal and unequal, believe that what they have in common has greater value in the formation of a good community. Conversely, those who are not egalitarian, while starting from the same premise, believe that

> their diversity has greater value in the formation of a good community.[21]

The inequality that the right finds pleasing to the eye, because it sees therein a mirror of natural design, outrages the left as a fluke of history.

Thus the right tends to wrap itself in the legitimacy of tradition, while the left puts its trust in the artifice of reason. As Bobbio says, "The right is more willing to accept the natural and that second nature constituted by custom, tradition and force of the past." The left, on the other hand, can find no reason to be inclined to sustain the habit of centuries. Its conviction lies in the effectiveness of human action in transforming the world. The naturalism of the right contrasts with the artificialism of the left. Nothing further from leftist thought than a cult to tradition, than being enthralled by rites and ancestral practices merely because they are ancient. Nothing more anathema to the left than the pretension that differences should be perpetuated, shielded behind custom. The left is, at the same time, a project of equality and a project of reason.

Equality and reason. This may very well be the formula of Bobbian leftism. An ideal and a method: fraternity and common sense. The left Bobbio believes in must be, therefore, as alien to exclusion as it is to fanaticism. The lay spirit is the spark plug that the left must not deny, at the risk of denying itself. From his indispensable laicism come his essential impulses: commitment to critical rigor, rejection of dogmatism, disdain for demagoguery, censor-

[21] Norberto Bobbio, *Left and Right* (Chicago, Illinois: University of Chicago Press, 1997), pp. 66-67.

ship of superstition. Bobbio cannot help but see the left as the most faithful child of the enlightenment. Perhaps this is one of his most persistent contributions: from the dense decay of his pessimism, two beacons can be discerned: equality and reason.

Old age caused the philosopher to turn his gaze toward himself. A man dedicated to providing commentary on the classics, who used his teaching as a platform to orient contemporary debate, looked to his own experience. This shift was odd. His political philosophy was a self-denial of sorts, because it always went hand-in-hand with the classics. Don't listen to me, heed the warnings of Machiavelli, the proposals of Constant, the logic of John Stuart Mill. His ordering intelligence can scarcely be heard, like the voice of someone interpreting the ideas of others. And yet after he turned eighty, Bobbio started to distance himself from academia and approach his own experience. Once someone who delighted in concepts, he now discovered himself savoring affections in his old age. And thus, Bobbio gradually gave way to the temptation to talk about himself.

In his essay on old age, he writes, "The world of old people, all old people, is to a greater or lesser extent the world of memory."[22] Affections devoured by time, places visited in remote years, fragments of poetry memorized in adolescence, scenes from movies and novels. Friends, family, loves. But old age is terrible. Even memory, its only treasure, begins to wander. It drags its feet, falls behind,

[22] Norberto Bobbio, *Old Age and Other Essays* (Cambridge, Oxford, and Malden: Polity Press, 2001). p. 12.

repeats itself, becomes boring. There is a lush literary tradition that praises old age. Advertising wants to turn old age into wrinkled little old men, wise and smiling, happy to still be walking around. They are not called old men, but "senior citizens." What these messages are trying to do is turn old age into new merchandise, a new clientele. Old age is terrible. He who praises old age has not looked it in the face, he says, paraphrasing Erasmus. It is enough to see the pain of hospitals, the loneliness of old age homes, the despair of the sick. Bobbio knew from experience that old age is ugly and moreover, lasts an eternity. A whole life behind you. The end has arrived. The elderly have no future and ahead lies death. Bobbio faced it without hope. "As a layman," he would say, "I live in a world in which the dimension of hope is unknown." Death is the end, an entry into the world of non-being.

In the epilogue of *The Maker*, Borges portrays an old man. "A man took it upon himself to draw the world. For years he filled a space with images of provinces, kingdoms, mountains, bays, ships, islands, fish, rooms, instruments, stars, horses, and people. Not long before he died, he discovered that this patient labyrinth of lines formed the image of his own face." Bobbio, a man who proposed to portray the world of politics, drew onto its countenance the image of meekness. This was his most beloved virtue, and he dedicated one of his final essays to it.

Ernesto Treccani, a friend of his, organized a cycle of conferences in order to compile a dictionary of virtues. Asked to contribute, Bobbio immediately chose meekness. The dictionary was never completed, but the essay made it into print. *Elogio della mitezza* was the title in Italian.

It is difficult to translate *mitezza* into English. The word can mean tameness, although the term seems to be more applicable to animals than to men. *Mitezza* is temperance, moderation, flexibility, sweetness, ductility, gentleness.

Bobbio was not inclined to discuss virtues. A modern disciple of Hobbes, wary of bombastic Republican rhetoric, Bobbio did not believe that coexistence could ever be sustained on the pillars of good will. The corpulence of a punishing State could lend meaning to coexistence, not the call of morality. Given the ethics of virtue, the skeptic decidedly embraced the ethics of rules. The Bobbio of final confidences touched on what his theory had ignored. The cartographer spoke thus of the virtue he loved most. Not as if it were the moral attribute par excellence, as if moderation were the queen of human virtues. For him, it was something more modest but far more loveable: the cloak donned by a dubitative character. Bobbio explores moderation as if he were writing one of the unwritten chapters of the *Critique of Myself* he once wanted to publish, as a tribute to Croce.

There are those who have chosen to see the thousands of scattered papers by Bobbio, the scores of conferences, presentations, and seminars, as an effort to construct a general theory of politics. This is, precisely, the name of the anthology his disciple Bovero compiled. It is debatable that this was the objective of the Bobbian *opus*, but in any case, the noteworthy aspect of his reflection on meekness is that it positions itself in the terrain of the apolitical. Mine, Bobbio says, is the most anti-political of virtues. Rather than praise, meekness draws the Prince's scorn: to say gentle is to say weak, vacillating, irresolute. The lamb is a docile, martirized animal; not like the fox or the lion, Machiavelli's favorite beasts. Hence the attraction: "One cannot cultivate political philosophy without trying to understand what is beyond politics, or without venturing into the non-political sphere, and attempting to establish the boundaries between the political and the non-political."

But what is this gentleness Bobbio praises, this meekness he identifies with? It is, above all, the opposite of arrogance.

> A meek person does not have a high opinion of himself, not because of a lack of self-esteem, but due to his propensity to believe more in the lowly rather than the lofty nature of humankind, and because he shares that humanity... The meek, instead, 'let others be themselves' irrespective of whether these individuals may be arrogant, haughty, or domineering. They do not engage with others intending to compete, harass, and ultimately prevail. They refrain from exercising the spirit of contest, competition, or rivalry, and therefore also of winning. In life's struggle meek persons are perpetual losers.[23]

Bobbio is wrong on this last point. Meekness is to man what ductility is to solid bodies. The meek are not "perpetual losers" because they never have to compete. They can pass through the flame without being burned.

But even meekness finds its limit, its final curtain. Bobbio stated as much in his tardy confession: "I loath fanatics with all my soul."

---

[23] Norberto Bobbio, *In Praise of Meekness: Essays on Ethics and Politics* (Cambridge, Oxford, and Malden: Polity Press, 2000). pp. 28-29.

Tragic Liberalism

Pity that the only way to paradise is in a hearse.

Stanislaw Lec

When they met in New York, Greta Garbo stared at him long and hard. Then the melancholy diva greeted him briefly in her thick voice, managing only to say, "You have beautiful eyes." Hidden behind the round windows of his glasses, the professor's were dark, vivid, penetrating. Perhaps the actress who made the fearsome beauty of Mata Hari come to life was able to see many gazes, many men, many centuries peering out of that timid visage. They were the eyes of an intelligence capable of viewing the world from opposing perspectives, the eyes of a man whose own vantage point was never enough. Marcel Proust once wrote that the only true voyage "consists not in seeking new landscapes, but in having new eyes; in seeing the universe through the eyes of another, one hundred others –in seeing the hundred universes that each of them sees." Berlin made of his life a true voyage in this sense. He saw the world as Machiavelli or Kant would see it, as Dostoyevsky or Tolstoy, Marx or Mill, fox or hedgehog. Berlin saw history through the eyes of many.

When he looked in the mirror, Berlin saw an "impossibly ugly" man. His habit of belittling himself originated, perhaps, with his own displeasure over the shape of his body: an elephant with narrow shoulders and clumsy arms. That is why Greta Garbo's flirtatious comment left him speechless: the lecturer was accustomed to dodging other kinds of praise. Meeting him for the first time, his eyes were not what captured one's attention. What captivated his interlocutors was his voice: his accent, his diction, how quickly he could string together long phrases as if they were the letters of an interjection. One of his high school teachers marveled at his conversation: it was as if instead of talking, he were playing an instrument. Not a flute that sang in search of beauty, but rather one that savored the pleasure of making sounds. Like a fountain. No friend, no disciple, no colleague of his would fail to retain his breakneck speech as a lasting memory. Berlin's voice, galloping onward without pause. He was, as one of his Oxford professors recalled, the only man who pronounced the word "epistemological" as a single syllable. When Joseph Brodsky began his exile in London, he heard Isaiah Berlin's voice on the other end of the telephone line; the admired author of essays on freedom was talking at the most extraordinary speed. It was, the great Russian poet would remember, as if the speed of sound were pursuing the speed of light.[1]

Berlin's words came in quick succession at unheard of speed, but without tripping over each other. In his speech

[1] Josephy Brodsky, "Isaiah Berlin: A Tribute," in Edna Ullmann-Margalit and Avisahai Margalit, Eds., *Isaiah Berlin. A Celebration* (Chicago, Illinois: The University of Chicago Press, 1991).

without breath or pause, the thread of reason was neatly spooled. Behind that hurried voice lay the serenity of a musical score. This can be heard in recordings of his conferences. The flow of his words is fiery and at times, dark, but his speed does not lead to imprecision or stumbling. Every exposition is clad in perfect armor. Each proposal is delineated, all the main ideas drawn up, any objections examined, a thesis finally formulated. In his racing voice, no phrase is left without an ending, nor does any idea fail to reach its conclusion. Every parenthesis has its opening and closure. This is why those who attended his legendary conferences, or who heard the professor's radio broadcasts, marveled at the melodic grace of his words and the symphonic architecture of his intelligence.

But his voice also carried a third frame: the strata of his accent. Berlin would come to embody the prototypical gentleman: elegant, cultured, punctilious, and mild. The suit was always three-piece. But this most English of Englishmen was also an outsider: the least English of Englishmen.[2] This tension could be perceived in his voice. Blended on the gentleman's palate were the layers of his own self. As his biographer, Michael Ignatieff, said: "The genealogy of his vocal mannerisms is the story of how all the layers of his identity settled into his voice."[3] Slav and Jewish sonorities melted into the modulations of the British intellectual aristocracy.

---

[2] He is described thus by Ian Buruma, who recalls his friend: "The Last Englishman," in *Anglomania. A European Love Affair* (New York: Vintage Books, 1998).

[3] Michael Ignatieff, *Isaiah Berlin. A Life* (New York: Metropolitan Books, 1998), p. 3.

Isaiah Berlin was born on June 6, 1909 in Riga, a Baltic city that would later become the capital of Latvia –at the time, it formed part of the Tsarist empire. His birth was considered a miracle. A few years earlier, his mother had delivered a stillborn baby, and the doctors had handed down the verdict that she would never become a mother. Now there were further complications. After long hours of tension and anguish overshadowed by death, the doctor took the forceps and pulled the baby's left arm with such force, his ligaments were damaged permanently.[4]

An only child, Isaiah would live closely attached to his parents in that small city on the outskirts of an empire. Mendel, his father, was an intelligent, unassuming Jewish merchant. Marie, his mother, was a round, petite woman who adored the Italian opera. When he was seven years old, the family moved to Saint Petersburg. Like John Stuart Mill, Isaiah did not attend school. He learned from the books in his home. His education was nourished by the family library, located on the top floor of a ceramics factory. His lack of a formal education did not significantly limit his learning. By the time he was ten, he had already read *War and Peace* and *Anna Karenina*. As he studied Hebrew and the Talmud, he also dove into the stories of Jules Verne and the musketeers of Dumas. There was a lot of reading, and not much play.

In the winter of 1917, the three Berlins were drawn to the windows of their home by a commotion rising from the streets. The din gradually became clearer: "Power to the Duma," "Land and Liberty," "Down with the Tsar."

---

[4] All biographical references come from Ignatieff's book, by far the best reconstruction of Berlin's life.

Mendel and Marie took part in the general excitement: they saw masses clamoring for justice, crying out against despotism. A few days later, when things seemed to have calmed down, their seven-and-a-half year old son went out into the street. He was on his way to buy a book by Jules Verne when he came across a group of men dragging along someone who had fallen prey to the revolt. He was a municipal police officer, unmasked by the revolutionaries. The scene passed quickly before the eyes of a boy who probably guessed that the man these rebels were dragging off would not escape with his life. The boy's imagination foreshadowed what was to come: the annihilation of a man in the hands of hatred. The scene was tattooed on Isaiah Berlin's memory. Soon Isaiah's parents discovered that the liberal revolution had evolved into something very different. They saw in Lenin the convictions of a dangerous fanatic.

By 1919, the Berlin family had been compelled by the housing committee to vacate any rooms not being used in their apartment. Occupied by strangers, their home was no longer theirs. The atmosphere gradually became hostile: frequent searches, privations, fear. On one occasion, their rooms were sacked by the secret police in search of jewels. That was when the family decided to leave Bolshevik Russia. Mendel Berlin was not willing to bear the sensation of being invaded in his own home: the isolation, the constant espionage, the capricious arrests, and the feeling of impotence caused by the madness of the men who led the coup.

In October 1920, they left Saint Petersburg. After a brief stay in Riga, they would make their home in England, the island idealized by the paterfamilias as a citadel of true civilization. His son would inherit this love for all things British. For Isaiah Berlin, England was the rock from which the principles he held dear had sprung, where tolerance and respect for others had germinated. This was where the rule of law had taken hold. An island that, unlike the continent, had never embraced fanaticism; a land that valued liberty over efficiency and prized the sweetness of certain incoherencies over the rough-hewn order of dogmatism.

The boy would quickly adapt to city, school, and language. He won a scholarship that made it possible for him to enroll in Oxford, England's oldest university, where he would later teach. By 1933, as an unknown professor who had published a few articles on music in student journals, he received an assignment to write an essay on Karl Marx. Berlin was not the editors' first choice for this collection of university texts. They had already sought out Sidney and Beatrice Webb and Harold Laski, all of whom had rejected the proposal. Berlin accepted without knowing much about the figure in question and without feeling any attraction whatsoever for the edifice he had built. In fact, Marx was the origin of a regime he loathed. At college he had tried to read *Das Kapital*, but found the prose intolerable. Writing about Marx, thus, was the only way of getting to know him. And so Berlin spent five years in the company of a man whom he found rather unpleasant.

He learned to appreciate him or at the very least, to understand him. The result of this youthful endeavor is a book in which all the luminous signs of his mature work can be found. In this brief portrait, Marx's ideas come to life. They are not blocks of granite, but pulsations obeying a vital drive. Berlin entered classrooms where Marx had studied philosophy in Berlin, read his early works, retraced his trip to Paris in order to admire his polemic talent and feel out the underpinnings of his friendships and rivalries, registered his literary tastes and his states of mind, followed his footsteps during a long day of London exile. His vision of history, understanding of economics, and anticipation of the future do not appear as slabs of bronze, but as derivations of an extraordinary intelligence. Berlin never had any interest in economics, much less Marxist economics. In fact, he always felt deeply mistrustful of the social sciences. He saw them as vain, uncouth mumbo jumbo. What he was interested in was the making of ideas, the fascinating life of thought. In order to understand Marx, Berlin acts as a reporter who registers the conflicts, the alliances, the struggles of his existence; a busybody who scrutinizes private papers and letters, a novelist who describes atmospheres in great detail and imagines the reasons behind actions being taken, an interpreter who weaves together the fragments of Marx's work in order to leave behind a more vivid picture of his thought, a lawyer who defends his client from the accusations of his enemies, and a critic who exhibits the weaknesses and dangers inherent in his ideas.

It is true that there are gaping holes in this essay.[5] Sixty years after it was published, one cannot say it provides the best gateway to Karl Marx's philosophy. No matter: the text is an extraordinary threshold into Berlin's universe. In his

[5] For a critical and at the same time respectful reading of Berlin's work, see the essay by G.A. Cohen, "Isaiah's Marx's and Mine," in the tribute anthology edited by the Margalits.

book, the capacity of the historian of ideas to appreciate the constituent features of a personality and examine the way in which his life was braided into his work can be fully appreciated. Despite the fact that Marx never kept a journal, that he was a man reluctant to speak of himself, Berlin seems to know him intimately as he describes him in his isolation, his introspection, and his aversion to mirrors. He appreciates the man of genius who was never fit for social leadership. He praises an intelligence that would not sell out to applause. He admires his imperturbable strength over the course of forty years of tribulation, illness and privation. Yet he is also irritated by the irascible man given to thunderclaps of fury, the arrogant polemicist who beat his critics to a pulp. He recognizes the talented writer, the ingenious pamphleteer who was deflated the moment he opened his mouth before an auditorium. Berlin not only exposes Marx's ideas, he also unpacks the intelligence they arise from: an active, practical mind that was not tempted by sentiment, its reason repudiating the hollow rhetoric of frauds and the idiotic conformism of the bourgeoisie.

The general feel of the essay is, beyond a doubt, critical. A secretary who was taking dictation from him suddenly exclaimed, "You don't seem to like Mr. Marx."[6] No, he didn't. But we find in Berlin an effort to understand the world just as it was seen by a figure he found essentially distasteful. This was precisely the gist of his method: in order to understand our reality, it is indispensable to expand oneself and view it from different angles. He who

[6] *Flourishing. Letters 1928-1946*, Ed. Henry Hardy (London: Chatto & Windus, 2004), p. 271.

sees the world only through the window shades of his eyelids loses sight of his back. Therefore, it is essential to find more than one way to observe the world. By seeing it through the eyes of both poet and engineer, rebel and tycoon, loyalist and traitor.

During World War II, Isaiah Berlin became the British government's retina in the United States. First he was stationed in New York, then in Washington, D.C. at the service of the British Embassy. His job was to file a weekly report on the climate of public opinion in the United States. He felt, Ignatieff says, the appetite for gossip and intrigue that make a good journalist –or a good diplomat, one might add. His conversational charm opened many doors. In the United States, during his daily encounters with officials, congressmen, journalists, businessmen, and union leaders, the image of him that they would come to admire was honed. It was spiced up with a sense of opportunity and preemptive duty. His ability to decipher the labyrinths of political life in the United States were born out of reason and memory, intuition and instinct.

Berlin's talents allowed him to quickly dominate a complex political labyrinth in a city of backroom intrigues, disputes, and lobbying wars. Sponge that he was, Berlin soaked up conversations, newspapers, inside information, intuitions, then squeezed them all out into his weekly report to London. The diplomat who never liked wielding a pen dictated his assessments. Secretaries worked miracles make his galloping language comprehensible. These diplomatic reports impressed the officials who read them back on the other side of the Atlantic.

Berlin described in vivid detail the complex relationship between the President and Congress as well as the atmosphere of U.S. public opinion, anticipating facts by intuiting the direction public life was taking. Among his most avid readers was Churchill himself, who considered the weekly bulletin pleasant reading material during the war. "The summaries are certainly well written. I have a feeling that they make the most of everything and present a somewhat perfervid picture of American affairs," he said.

In February 1944, Clementine Churchill commented to her husband that Irving Berlin, the composer of *There's No Business Like Show Business*, was in London and asked him if he would have time to visit with him. The Primer Minister caught only his last name and, recalling the admirable reports that were rolling in from Washington, responded immediately: by all means, have him come to lunch with us. And so Mr. Berlin was invited to dine on Downing Street with the Prime Minister. Terrified by the intensity of the political conversation, the composer remained silent for almost the entire meal. At one point, the Prime Minister addressed him to ask when he thought the war would end. "Mr. Prime Minister," the musician replied, "I shall tell my children and grandchildren that Winston Churchill asked *me* that question." Confused, Churchill asked his guest which was the most important work he had ever written. After hesitating for a moment, Berlin replied: "*White Christmas*."

In Washington and New York, Berlin discovered the world of power. And far from feeling repelled by the clash of ambitions, by the hypocrisy and simulation, he was fascinated by the greatness of these men of State. He knew the kind of politics found in the libraries of Oxford, in the books of Aristotle, Machiavelli and Montesquieu; the politics of treatises on justice and speculations regarding the origins of Society. Now he came into contact with the politics of power, the politics of decisions. It was living history: history on the march.

For five years he tried to decipher a world that was no longer wrapped up in speculating over the classics, but over the maneuvers of the living. Over eyes and language and temperaments; over tenacity of characters, movements, and reflections. No one who saw politics from up close could go on thinking this was the result of "vast, impersonal forces," as T.S. Eliot once said, a quote Berlin would use as the epigraph for one of his most celebrated essays. Politics, or rather History, walked hand in hand with specific men who were confronting their circumstances. He realized that more than all those hours in the library, what enabled him to understand the enigmas of real politics was his training in a disparaged art: gossip. In one of his letters to his parents, Isaiah Berlin confides that both his interest in understanding U.S. politics and his capacity to decipher its code sprang from his fascination with the lives of others. Institutions, he says in reference to U.S. political machinery, play an infinitely lesser role than we naïvely give them credit for. Despite the fact that we seek the rule of law, all governments are ruled by men. It is precisely individuals and the relationships between them that define, at the end of the day, the pathways of power. Far more than the fixed framework of rules, or the climate of culture, what counts is the melodrama of personalities. The characters of protagonists, their quarrels and affections, their qualities and scars are key.

He especially admired Churchill and Roosevelt, the Atlantic allies. Berlin composed memorable praise of this pair. His respect can be gleaned from his letters. On January 2, 1942, he detected a common thread between them. At a time when individuals find themselves incapable of appreciating the magnitude of the events that surround them, it is fortunate to find two men who feel at home with history.[7] Churchill was the man who possessed an historic imagination, the statesman who knew how to accommodate both present and future over the long loom of centuries. In archaic Churchillian rhetoric, Berlin caught a glimpse of a fresh, new tradition. The Baroque form of expression, the epic dimension of his call to blood, to sweat and, above all, to tears, succeeded in transmitting the sense of historic urgency that the moment called for. Berlin paints a superhuman statesman: "one of the two greatest men of action his nation has produced, an orator of prodigious powers, the saviour of his country, a mythical hero who belongs to legend as much as to reality, the largest human being of our time."[8] No less.

Roosevelt, unlike Churchill, was a man of the New Century and the New World, unafraid of the future. A spontaneous man, unorganized perhaps, who knew how to reconcile the seemingly incompatible. This was the great feat of the U.S. President: to defend fundamental

---

[7] *Flourishing...*, p. 391.

[8] "Winston Churchill in 1940," in *The Proper Study of Mankind*, Ed. Henry Hardy (New York: Farrar, Straus & Giroux, 2000), p. 627. When Churchill read the essay in a copy of the *Atlantic Monthly*, he grunted: "Too good to be true."

values without sacrificing others that were just as important. His service to humanity, Berlin says, was to teach us that it is possible to combine efficiency and kindness. He strengthened democracy by demonstrating that the advance of social justice and individual freedoms do not compromise efficient government. He transformed thus our idea of a government's obligations to its citizens: the moral responsibility of guaranteeing a minimum of social consideration.

In his essay on Roosevelt, Berlin sketches the portrait of two politicians. The first is tenacious; the second, adaptable. The former intends to impose his power onto circumstances; the latter molds himself to them. "The first kind of statesman," Berlin said, "is essentially a man of single principle and fanatical vision. Possessed by his own bright, coherent dream, he usually understands neither people nor events. He has no doubts or hesitations and by concentration of will-power, directness and strength he is able to ignore a great deal of what goes on outside him." His clarity, his determination, even his blindness can help him overcome resistance and bend men to his will. The other kind of statesman is doted with an acute sensitivity that allows him "to take in minute impressions, to integrate a vast multitude of small evanescent unseizable detail, such as artists possess in relation to their material." This politician is sculptor who heeds his materials. He does not see the world as black and white, nor does he believe that his task is a crusade with no distractions or delays. On the contrary, he knows that at times in order to move forward, one must beat around the bush, waiting for a riper moment, or even going against one's original purpose. There are doctrinaire politicians, and then there are intuitive ones.

A year or two after publishing his essay on the New Deal President, Isaiah Berlin gave a lecture in which he somehow returned to the subject of the statesman and the Machiavellian enigma par excellence: political efficacy. In a BBC broadcast from June 1957, he asked himself plainly: what does it mean to have good judgment in politics? What is it to have political wisdom, to be endowed for politics, to be a political genius, or perhaps simply to be politically competent, to know how to get things done? What is the science or art that politicians must become familiar with? Hobbes and his heirs have sustained that the statesman must know the mechanics of society in order to govern. Just as a technician needs to dominate the rules of his trade, the statesman must understand the anatomy of collective bodies, the molecular physics of individuals, the chemistry of collective passions, or the mechanics of political economy. No matter what the nature of this privileged science of society, common knowledge dictates that such a science does exist, and that the dominion of its laws is a basic requirement for an illustrated, effective government. The former leads to the latter.

A wise statesman is not a man of science, Berlin replies. If I am a ruler tortured by a complex decision, what good does it do me to compile all the information contained in libraries, what use are the lessons of historical philosophy, or the manuals of political economy?

> Obviously what matters is to understand a particular situation in its full uniqueness, the particular men and events and dangers, the

> particular hopes and fears which are actively at work in a particular place at a particular time: in Paris in 1791, in Petrograd in 1917, in Budapest in 1956, in Prague in 1968 or in Moscow in 1991.[9]

It does us no good to know some sort of law about the emergence of revolutions, formulated by a shrewd social scientist. What matters is our ability to comprehend a circumstance that, by definition, is unique. Political judgment is more reflex than reflection.

Skill trumps reason. What makes some politicians successful is that they do not think in abstract or general terms: their talent lies in their capacity to isolate the combination of elements that comprise *their* circumstances. That is why we speak of sound political vision, or sense of smell, or touch: sensible virtues, not intelligence. Above all else, the great statesman has a feel for the texture of the moment. Theoretical knowledge, erudition, and the power of abstract reasoning do little good: skill is everything. Berlin calls the shrewdness of Bismarck, Talleyrand, and Roosevelt "practical wisdom." We might call it *astuteness*: the intelligence of the hunter, the cook, the navigator. Astuteness is more synthetic than analytic; it is far-sighted and agile. More than profound, it is prudent. *Clever intelligence* is a combination of "flair, sagacity, foresight, adaptability, pretense, resourcefulness, vigilance, opportunism."[10]

---

[9] "Political Judgement," in *The Sense of Reality. Studies in Ideas and their History* (New York: Farrar, Strauss & Giroux, 1996), pp. 44-45.

[10] Thus it is summed up by Marcel Detienne and Jean-Pierre Vernant, quoted by François Jullien in *A Treatise on Efficacy* (Honolulu: University of Hawaii Press, 2004), p. 7.

Political wisdom is not derived from a concept, but from experience. Political judgment needs no theories to examine circumstance, that complex and unrepeatable platform of the present. Political prudence lies in an elemental registry of the territory one is traversing and of that which lies latent underneath. Churchill heard the murmuring of centuries past; Roosevelt caught a whiff of the future. In both cases, the present is burdened with messages: it is never just the present. The statesman examines acting forces, powers in play, synergies in motion. The important thing is not to view circumstances as if they were set in stone. Confronted by syllogisms, all that matters is opportunity, the convergence of action and time. Good politics are good only at the right moment.

During the summer of 1945, while still in the service of the British Embassy in Washington, Isaiah Berlin was informed that he would be transferred to Moscow for several months. The Embassy was understaffed and needed the support of someone who spoke Russian. The war had just ended and the relationship between these former allies was governed by optimism. Berlin had not been in Russia since 1919, when he was just ten years old. He was excited about returning, but the trip also swathed him in fear. He had a recurring nightmare that Soviet police would arrest him and prevent him from leaving the country. His work at the chancellorship was not particularly distinguished: he had to read the Soviet press and comment on its contents. The media in Moscow lacked the richness it had in England or the United States. The monotony of propaganda permeated every column. The newspapers didn't have much juice to squeeze out, and the party bureaucrats were talking into the microphones that were embedded everywhere, rather than to their interlocutors. Berlin had a lot of free time. He visited museums, historic buildings, theaters, bookstores, libraries.[11]

The professor had been warned that it would be difficult to contact Soviet citizens, much less intellectuals. The doors would always be open of bureaucrats who repeated the official party line, but artists were encouraged not to speak to foreigners. Yet Berlin was spirited enough to raise the curtain that had been lowered in front of diplomats. His charming conversation elicited the affections of extraordinary writers and artists. The thirty-something-year-old diplomat was able to get to know the vivid cultural scene of the Soviet Union very well, one that had been quashed by the founding of a police regime. Experimentation during the 1920's in cinema, fiction, painting, and theater had been followed by fear.

Two poets he met on this voyage would mark Berlin's life: Boris Pasternak and Anna Akhmatova. He had known and admired Pasternak's work for quite some time, and there was no trouble looking him up because he had brought along a pair of boots that Pasternak's sisters, Berlin's neighbors at Oxford, had sent him. Pasternak was soon captivated by this brilliant reader of his work who had come from England bearing gifts. Pasternak told him

[11] The texts Berlin drafted during his visits to the Soviet Union were compiled into *The Soviet Mind. Russian Culture under Communism*, published by the Brookings Institution and edited by Henry Hardy, with a prologue by Strobe Talbott (Washington, D.C.: 2004).

of his participation in the Anti-fascist Congress in Paris in 1935. During his presentation, he had simply said:

> I understand that this is a meeting of writers to organise resistance to Fascism. I have only one thing to say to you about that. Do not organise. Organisation is the death of art. Only personal independence matters. In 1789, 1848, 1917 writers were not organised for or against anything; do not, I implore you, do not organise.[12]

Berlin became his window to the West, a land he knew nothing about. The pleasure of bearing news from the outside world to people so eager to receive it was for the visitor an indescribable emotion: it was like "speaking to the victims of shipwreck on a desert island, cut off for decades from civilization – all they heard, they received as new, exciting and delightful."

Berlin describes Pasternak as a genius who created poetry not only in his poems, but in everything else he did as well. And what is genius? He asked himself. To make what others find impossible look easy. To stop in mid-air when one leaps without having to fall immediately back down to the ground, as the ballet dancer Nijinsky would say. To remain up in the air before landing. Berlin struck up a close relationship with Pasternak. He visited him every week. They spoke of books and authors, of the terrible conditions under the Stalin era. During an encounter some time later, Pasternak would take him to his study and hand him a thick envelope

[12] In "Meeting with Russian Writers in 1945 and 1956," in *Personal Impressions* (Princeton, New Jersey: Princeton University Press, 2001), p. 214.

with a manuscript. He said to him: "My book. It's all there. These are my last words. Please, read it." It was *Doctor Zhivago*.

He met Anna Akhmatova by pure coincidence. The diplomat, saturated with free time, would troll used bookstores in Saint Petersburg, the city he knew as a child. He found it had changed a lot: a war and a revolution stood between his presence and his memories. In one of these bookstores, Berlin started up a conversation with a man he saw leafing through a book of poetry. He turned out to be a literary critic. When he questioned him about Leningrad writers, the man asked him: do you mean Akhmatova? Berlin had heard the poet's name, but he didn't know much about her work. He had her placed as a great poet of yesteryear. She had been blacklisted since 1925. He thought she was dead. But Akhmatova was not only alive; her house was a few blocks away from the used bookstore. The critic offered to telephone her and make the necessary introductions. She said she would receive them both at three o'clock that same afternoon.

Berlin arrived punctually at Akhmatova's home. He climbed the dark stairways and entered the room. The apartment was modestly furnished. There were no rugs or curtains. The original furniture was no longer there. Had it been stolen? Had she sold it? A table, a few rickety chairs, a sofa, and a beautiful portrait of her drawn by Modigliani. Then she appeared: the greatest Russian poet of the 20th century. Berlin described her as a "stately, grey-haired" woman. A "tragic queen" who moved about slowly, with great dignity. Her handsome, sorrowful features, her severe, yet gentle expression. Joseph Brodsky, a mutual friend, evoked her presence thus, a few years before her hair turned gray: "She looked positively stunning. Five feet eleven, dark-haired, fair-skinned, with pale gray-green eyes like those of snow leopards, slim and incredibly lithe..."[13] The encounter was quickly interrupted by Randolph Churchill, who was in town and wanted to use Isaiah as an interpreter. Berlin had to leave, but they agreed to take up the conversation where they had left off later that night.

He returned at nine in the evening. She was accompanied by a friend who left around midnight. Then, once again, the same phenomenon he had experienced with Pasternak: the need to absorb all possible information from the messenger who had come from the West. They also talked about writers and literature. But they spoke of more intimate affairs as well. She told him of her loves. Of the poet Mandelstam, who had been head over heels with her. Of her friendship with Modigliani. Of her infancy on the shores of the Black Sea. Of her first husband, the poet Gumilyov, of his failures and his execution in 1921, accused of an attempt on Lenin's life. She spoke to him about her son's arrest, or rather, disappearance. Of the long months waiting for news of him. The conversation was accompanied by pauses and tears.

She asked him if he would like to hear her poems. She recited from memory fragments of *Réquiem*, the poem she wrote over the course of twenty years after the Soviet police arrested her son a second time: he was finally freed after it was determined that his "sentence

[13] *Less than One: Selected Essays* by Joseph Brodsky (New York: Farrar, Straus & Giroux, 1986), p. 36.

was unjustified." For years, there was no written registry of the poem. The mere possession of its lines was a death sentence. Eleven people knew it by heart and had preserved it through recitation. The funeral mass names both the victims of totalitarian horror and those who loved torture, the experts in manufacturing orphans. They are all in the poem: the pregnant poet from whom the police kick out a stillborn son; the hanged friend; the man who, feeling betrayed, shoots himself; the dishonored poet who denounces his lover; the years in concentration camps; the neighbor who throws himself out of the window rather than accuse his friend.

> I should like to call you all by name,
> but they have lost the lists....
>
> I have woven for them a great shroud
> Out of the poor words I overheard them speak.

Akhmatova names her own torment, the torment of women whose children, parents, siblings, husbands were torn away from them by the powers that be.

> They took you away at daybreak. Half waking, as though at a wake, I followed.
> In the dark chamber children were crying,
> In the image-case, candlelight guttered.
> At your lips, the chill of an ikon,
> A deathly sweat at your brow.
> I shall go creep to our wailing wall,
> Crawl to the Kremlin towers.

The poet interrupted her reading with memories. Her husband and her son arrested, tortured in concentration camps. The women, week after week, month after month hoping for news. The silence of the prisons.

For seventeen months I've called you
To come home, I've pleaded
–O my son, my terror!–groveled
At the hangman's feet.
All is confused eternally–
So much, I can't say who's
Man, who's beast any more, nor even
How long until execution.
Simply the flowers of dust,
Censers ringing, tracks from a far
Settlement to nowhere's ice.
And everywhere the glad
Eye of a huge star's
Still tightening vice.

Berlin listed to a dry voice speak of the dementia of a century in which "only the dead smiled, glad to be at rest." There is no other task, she says, than to finish killing one's memory and turning one's soul into stone.

There I learned how faces fall apart,
How fear looks out from under the eyelids,
How deep are the hieroglyphics
Cut by suffering on people's cheeks.
There I learned how silver can inherit
The black, the ash-blond, overnight,

The smiles that faded from the poor in spirit,
Terror's dry coughing sound.

The night wore on. It was already three in the morning. She brought a plate of boiled potatoes in from the kitchen. It was the only thing she had to offer him. The conversation continued. It branched off into Dostoyevsky and Tolstoy, Joyce and Eliot. She asked her guest about his personal life. He trustingly answered. They spoke of piano music by Beethoven, Bach, and Chopin. By then, the sunlight was streaming through the curtainless window. It was already eleven in the morning. Isaiah Berlin kissed Anna Akhmatova's hand and returned exalted to his hotel room. She wrote:

As if on the rim of a cloud
I remember your words,
And because of my words to you,
Night became brighter than day.
Thus torn from the earth,
We rose up, like stars.
There was neither despair nor shame,
Not now, not afterward, not at the time.
But in real life, right now,
You hear how I am calling you.
And that door that you half opened.
I don't have the strength to slam.

Sounds die away in the ether.
And darkness overtakes the dusk.
In a world become mute for all time,

There are only two voices, yours and mine.
And to the almost bell-like sound
Of the wind from invisible Lake Ladoga,
The late night dialogue turned into
The delicate shimmer of interlaced rainbows.[14]

That long conversation would haunt them both the rest of their days.[15] He would consider it the most intense moment of his life. For her it was the night that changed history. Not long after the encounter, the secret police visibly bugged the ceiling of Akhmatova's home. These were not instruments of espionage; they were devices of intimidation. The harassment continued. The party censored magazines that had published her poems, declaring her work the portrait of a lady fluttering between the convent and the bordello. Her poetry, the censors determined, was nothing more than an aristocratic blend of sadness, nostalgia, death, and damnation. The "half nun and half whore," according to the tyrant's insult, was expelled from the writers' union and her books, banned.

She was convinced that her night with Berlin was responsible for her disgrace. But she did not blame Isaiah for her fate. She thought it had been wrought thus by destiny. Isaiah Berlin was a "guest from the future." Not long

---

[14] From Judith Hemschemeyer's translation of *The Complete Poems of Anna Akhmatova* (Boston: Zephyr Press, 2000).

[15] Regarding this legendary encounter, we have more than Berlin's testimony and Ignatieff's blow-by-blow account. Hungarian writer György Dalos dedicated an entire book to the conversation: *The Guest from the Future. Anna Akhmatova and Isaiah Berlin* (New York: Farrar, Straus & Giroux, 1999). An opera based on the encounter between Berlin and Akhmatova premiered in July 2004, with music by Mel Marvin and a libretto by Jonathan Levi.

after she would write her third dedication for the "Poem without a hero":

> He will not be a beloved husband to me
> But what we accomplish, he and I,
> Will disturb the Twentieth Century.

She was certain that over the course of that evening, which lasted until eleven a.m., the Cold War was unleashed.

After this immersion in diplomacy, Isaiah Berlin returned to his ivory tower to enjoy what he called its sublime distance from the real world. He dedicated his life to teaching at Oxford and paraded through all the major U.S. universities, but he never became an academic recluse. Berlin was not a professor who addressed only his students and other professors. Far from being trapped in the library and the classroom, Berlin was a man who attracted the spotlight of fame. His philosophy and history classes at Oxford drew more and more students. He was soon known as the university's most attractive professor. The students who filled the auditoriums would recall his lessons as a ceremony and an adventure.

Out of his conferences, conversations, anecdotes, and texts, a legend grew. His erudition, his voice, the snails of his diction, and the clarity with which he was able to unravel a complex theme made him quite the character. His lessons escaped the confines of the classroom and entered barbershops via BBC broadcasts. T.S. Eliot praised his "torrential eloquence." Michael Oakeshott, upon introducing him at the London School of Economics, called him with a touch of scorn the "Paganini of the platform." Avishai Margalit crowned him king of adjectives: he could delve into the marrow of any figure using only the cadence of subtle expressions. If we pay heed to those who have shared the experience of listening to his conferences, one might call them a concert of ideas. Lelia Brodersen, who worked for a time as his secretary, described the enchantment of his dissertations. Berlin settled in behind the lectern, fixed his gaze on the back of the room and spoke with the speed of a popped cork. For an hour, not pausing for a second, Berlin spilled his eloquence over the auditorium. Without so much as catching his breath, the man moved like a pendulum, forward and backward. A "furious stream of words" would flow into "beautifully finished sentences." If at any time she had ever been in contact with true inspiration –she later recalled– it was with this virtuoso.[16]

Berlin had a gift for communicating simultaneously with many audiences. Connecting with philosophers and historians, he was also able to reach a vast auditorium. Academics discussed his interpretations, took advantage of his finds, discoursed regarding his proposals. Non-specialists enjoyed the ride. He was no vulgarizer, compressing ideas into junk food for quick consumption; nor was he an erudite, cut off within his own intellectual shire. His prose was never tangled up, never lost in abstraction, never buried in the details of an obsessed specialist.

To Berlin, the vitality of concepts was not to be found within the concepts themselves, but in the men who had

[16] The description is in Henry Hardy's prologue to *Freedom and Its Betrayal. Six enemies of human liberty* (Princeton, New Jersey: Princeton University Press, 2002). The book is a transcription of the conferences Berlin gave in 1952.

thought them up. The ideas that perennially fascinated him –the Enlightenment and anti-rationalism, national identity, fascism, the Romantic temperament and pluralism– never failed to encounter their emblematic biographies. His insurrection against the "tyranny of the concept" would lead this historian of ideas to become, instead, their biographer. If he wanted to examine the emergence of nationality, he chose to portray Herder, the poet and philosopher who understood the need to belong; while digging up the roots of fascism, he traced the silhouette of Joseph de Maistre; to color in the concept of liberty, he composed a gallery of his friends and enemies: Montesquieu, Mill, and Kant on one wall; Rousseau, Hegel, and Marx on the other. Ideas come to life through the lives of men. Ideas do not float: they breathe.

Eyes upon eyes. Man approaches the past, seeking the ways the men of yesteryear thought, felt, desired. Comprehension is not derived from any concept, but from a kind of cultivated fantasy. It is all about, as Berlin himself said, "imaginative insight." This is what nourishes understanding. Philosophy, the portraitist insinuated, must be connected to a poetic sentiment that allows one to entertain individual experience. Berlin could write about an obscure German thinker from the 19th century as if he were some fellow he had run into at a party the night before. His passion for ideas was spiced up by nosy curiosity, by his will to decipher the spirit of a character, the meaning of an instant, the core of an idea through a juicy, revealing anecdote.

His primary concern were his adversaries. Since his study of Marx, Berlin had explored the reasoning of anti-liberals, anti-modernists and anti-rationalists. Perhaps one of his best essays was the portrait he painted of Joseph de

Maistre. It would be hard to imagine a character further removed from our gentle liberal than this admirer of executioners. And yet, Berlin painted a full-body portrait of the furious reactionary who saw the world as a slaughterhouse. Reading one's allies is rather boring. It is far more interesting to read one's opponents; they put us to the test. That is what Berlin attempted: an ongoing reexamination of his convictions as an afflicted liberal through interpellation of his most energetic critics.

The biographer delves into his characters. He speaks through them. That is why it is hard to parse Berlin's philosophy. The source of his own ideas empties into the spring from which those of others emerge. Berlin appropriates his authors. He hides inside them. In his portraits, his brushstrokes remain visible. We are able to see, of course, the nose and forehead of his figures, their period costumes, the landscape of time that envelops them; yet the line, color, and texture of his canvasses are unequivocally his. In his rendering, the historian highlights only the ideas he finds most endearing, neglecting those that interest him the least. The portraitist does not need to gaze upon himself in the mirror to be reflected in each of his paintings. His Machiavelli, for example, is emblematic of this appropriation. The Florentine who appears in his gallery is not the cynical technician of power, the impassive advisor to the prince who is willing to recommend lies and death that favor the State. Nor is he the patriot, the passionate Republican who seeks first and foremost the unity of Italy. Berlin's Machiavelli is the pluralist who breaks away from the illusion of finding a sole principle capable of governing those lives. His Machiavelli is the revolutionary who stuck a sword into the consciousness of the Western world when he sliced through the code that attempted to regulate the lives of men. The author of *The Prince* appears as the man who shredded the fantasy of moral simplicity. In direct confrontation with the morality transmitted by the Church we find the morality demanded by the State. Machiavelli appears thus as an unconscious forerunner of pluralism, as well as a pioneer of liberal tolerance. Berlin's Machiavelli greatly resembles... Berlin himself. This did not escape the attention of critics of his work. It is why the scathing critic Christopher Hitchens, a man who never felt much sympathy for him, called him a skilled ventriloquist.

He did not like to be called a philosopher. He was a historian of ideas. And he became one because, when exploring the pathways of Western thought, he categorically refused to construct a system that would encompass the world, history, or mankind. Joseph Brodsky, who understood this very well, noted that philosophy can take on a totalitarian guise: the full structuring of ideas and concepts. Berlin's liberalism is born precisely out of his reluctance to comfortably order everything known to us. Brodsky read in Russia a pared-down version of the *Four Essays on Liberty*. In them he had encountered a precious anti-philosophy: the rejection of the all-encompassing globe. "What was good about *Four Essays on Liberty* was that it advanced none, since 'liberty' and 'system' are antonyms."[17]

While the observation of the Russian poet can be validated as a description of Berlin's fragmentary liberalism,

---

[17] Joseph Brodsky, "Isaiah Berlin: A Tribute," *op. cit.*, pp. 211-212.

it is by no means a description of liberalism, which has attempted to delineate a system through countless blueprints. Many a great liberal thinker has strived to shroud liberty with a coherent mantle of concepts, principles, and rules. Locke, Kant, John Stuart Mill, Popper, and Rawls sought logic in liberty, and they believed they had found it. They had their well-laid plans, comprised of norms. But unlike these philosophers of liberty, Berlin detested –as did Tocqueville– absolute systems that constituted an attempt to interweave all precepts of human coexistence. He believed, along with Herzen, whom he greatly admired, that a man can only observe the world freely when he is not compelled to accommodate the fronds of his gaze within the diagram of a theory.

Systematic liberals do, however, offer a key to putting the puzzle together. History is seen as an enigma that philosophy can resolve. At the end of the day, they trust that the fragmented canvas will be remedied by a constitution, or some ark of principles. The puzzle of history can be solved. This cavity can be made to fit around that protuberance. Every crest has its valley. Once the pieces fall into place, the big picture will become clear. There will be no gaps or bits left over. A sum total will emerge from the harmonic interlocking of fragments. For Berlin, on the other hand, there is no puzzle to decipher, because the pieces of our existence simply do not match up. Fragments are not complementary entities: they tend to disagree.

A few months after their wedding in the summer of 1956, Isaiah and his wife, Aline, settled down in a cabin at the small seaside town of Paraggi, on the Italian coast of Liguria. Isaiah enjoyed the isolation, the coastal breeze, splashing in the sea, and the food at the *trattorias*. Because of his weak left arm he could not swim, but he still enjoyed diving into the water. Over the following decade, they would spend practically all their summers there. Isaiah would set up shop every morning on the roof of the cabin. There, he worked on his most important conference and most polemic essay: "Two Concepts of Liberty." Over the two following summers, Berlin read, took notes, dictated into his recorder, corrected and restarted successive versions of this conference, seen as a golden opportunity to order his key convictions.

There are two kinds of people who speak of liberty, Berlin says. The first would like to limit the power that threatens them; the second would like to snatch it away from the oppressor. Thus, there are two concepts of liberty: negative and positive. No one has described negative liberty better than Hobbes did: as the absence of external impediments. I am free if I am left alone. The impulse toward negative liberty is born out of the desire that no one meddle with you. No matter if the busybody is a gendarme or a neighbor, a king or a mayor elected by the vote of the majority. Therefore, there is no logical connection between this liberty and any political regime. If we don't want power to disturb us, it matters not whether this power is monarchical or republican.

Positive freedom is born out of another impulse: the desire to be my own boss. Thus, positive freedom originates from an act of liberation from any outer or inner forces that keep me from being my own master. This emancipation is a victory over what ties me down, the passions that drive me mad, the ignorance that blinds me. It is a battle waged within myself. That is why the concept of positive liberty can act in such a way that enables those in power to justify coercion in the name of a higher freedom. Because of course a liberating power knows better than the individual what is best for him, what it is that subjugates him and how he must be freed.

Negative liberty is found in the walls that shield me, the curtains that protect me. Positive liberty lies in the power of an agent who succeeds in rescuing me from my illness, my madness, my raptures, or my poverty. One freedom defends the right to choose without obstacles; the other defends the right choice, molded to reason, justice, and truth. For some, freedom is having permission to be wrong, the right to be unhappy; for others, freedom is the empire of reason. "No one has rights against reason," Fichte said, outlining the parameters of positive liberty.

Truth be told, there wasn't much originality in the Berlinean defense of negative liberty. A long tradition, born out of Hobbes, that curiously enough has viewed liberty as the absence of obstructions. Constant, in his essay about the liberty of the moderns compared to that of the ancients, clearly distinguishes participation in public affairs from the liberty that shelters the private sector. Nor was there anything novel in Berlin's denunciation of the rhetorical traps of totalitarianism, cloaked in the defense of a higher liberty in order to crush another kind, despised as an unnecessary luxury. Karl Popper had already written his forceful allegation against Marxist historicism, and Talmon had denounced the totalitarian roots of Rousseauian democracy. What is notable about Berlin's argument, aside from his expressive elegance, is the accent he placed on the irremediable fragmentation of man. The three ideals of the French Revolution were precious, but incompatible. One cannot say: liberty, equality, fraternity. One must say: liberty, equality, or fraternity.

"Liberty is not the only goal of men," Berlin notes. When there are other deprivations, it can be reasonable to limit liberty.

> I am ready to sacrifice some, or all, of my freedom: I may do so willingly and freely; but it is freedom that I am giving up for the sake of justice or equality or the love of my fellow men. I should be guilt-stricken, and rightly so, if I were not, in some circumstances, ready to make this sacrifice. But a sacrifice is not an increase in what is being sacrificed, namely freedom, however great the moral need or the compensation for it. Everything is what it is: liberty is liberty, not equality or fairness or justice or culture, or human happiness or a quiet conscience. If the liberty of myself or my class or nation depends on the misery of a number of other human beings, the system which promotes this is unjust and immoral. But if I curtail or lose my freedom in order to lessen the shame of such inequality, and do not thereby materially increase the individual liberty of others, an absolute loss of liberty occurs.[18]

Liberty may be a precious value, but it is not the only value, or the ultimate value, or a value identical to all. At times, Berlin warns, liberty can become an obstacle to justice, security, and happiness. Politics, like life, is a

---

[18] Isaiah Berlin, "Two Concepts of Liberty" (New York: Farrar, Straus & Giroux, 1997), p. 197.

choice that encompasses all other values; in other words, a sacrifice. He states this very clearly at the end of the essay: the values of life are not only diverse, they tend to be incompatible. Thus, conflict and tragedy cannot ever be eliminated from human life. Every step we take is the abandonment of another path, every choice implies a loss. We cannot avoid the need to choose between our actions, goals, and values. Our values are in conflict. Such is our tragedy. We are broken inside, and we have no hope of repair. This is the fundamental note of Berlinean liberalism: its tragic significance.[19]

A deep Western optimism proclaims the compatibility of all values. Brandishing his trust in science, Condorcet said that Nature had joined together truth, virtue, and happiness with an indissoluble bond. All that is good goes together. Justice, beauty, friendship, equality, and freedom, locked in a fraternal embrace. Berlin asks whether this is true. His immediate response is no, it isn't. The good comes stuck to the bad. What is desirable is onerous. One good turn sacrifices another. No person can simultaneously possess all virtues. To opt for one is to renounce others. That was Machiavelli's original lesson: it is impossible to be a good man and a good prince at the same time. Whosoever would gain political glory must renounce heaven; whosoever seeks salvation must sacrifice his kingdom.

There is a pain in this somber liberalism that is more Russian than British. Every decision is steeped in sorrow, every step taken is somehow a disgrace. If the cosmic puz-

---

[19] See John Gray's essay, *Isaiah Berlin* (Princeton, New Jersey: Princeton University Press, 1997).

zle does not exist, if values and truths clash, if the right answers to our questions are contradictory, one cannot sensibly aspire to a definitive solution for our misfortune. We are burdened by the sacrificial nature of our decisions. And politics can aspire to nothing greater than the lesser evil. "We are doomed to choose, and every choice may entail an irreparable loss."[20] Those who live happily ever after, never feeling the stab of doubt, the pain implied in every choice, ignore the experience of being human.

The burden of liberty arises from our imperfections. Berlin, rather than lamenting this, welcomes it. Man is not, in the end, the perfect onion portrayed by Polish poet Wisława Szymborska:

> The onion, now that's something else.
> Its innards don't exist.
> Nothing but pure onionhood
> fills this devout onionist.
> Oniony on the inside,
> onionesque it appears.
> It follows its own daimonion
> without our human tears.
>
> Our skin is just a cover-up
> for the land where none dare go,
> an internal inferno,
> the anathema of anatomy.
> In an onion there's only onion

---

[20] Isaiah Berlin, "The Pursuit of the Idea," in *The Crooked Timber of Humanity* (New York: Alfred A. Knopf, 1991), p. 13.

from its tip to its toe,
onionymous monomania,
unanimous omninudity.

At peace, of a piece,
internally at rest.
Inside it, there's a smaller one
of undiminished worth.
The second holds a third one,
the third contains a fourth.
A centripetal fugue.
Polyphony compressed.

Nature's roundest tummy,
its greatest success story,
the onion drapes itself in its
own aureoles of glory.
We hold veins, nerves, fat,
secretions' secret sections.
Not for us such idiotic
onionoid perfections.[21]

Indeed, we have been denied the idiocy of perfection.

THE VENTRILOQUIST WAS ONCE ASKED WHOSE LIFE, OF all those he had portrayed, he would like to have lived. Berlin immediately responded: Herzen. From a very young age, Berlin marveled at the pen of the "Russian

[21] Wisława Szymborska, *Poems New and Collected*, trans. Stanislaw Baranczak and Clare Cavanagh (New York: Harvest, 2000), p. 166.

Voltaire." He was fascinated by the intense adventure of his life, amused by his malice, captivated by his wisdom, and hypnotized by long passages in his notebooks. There is no better guide to Berlin's convictions than the writings of Herzen. There is where we find what Berlin appreciates about himself. One of Herzen's contemporaries described thus the amazement of his conversation:

> This extraordinary mind which darted from one topic to another with unbelievable swiftness... He had a most astonishing capacity for instantaneous, unexpected juxtaposition of quite dissimilar things, and this gift he had in a very high degree, fed as it was by the powers of the most subtle observation and a very solid fund of encyclopedic knowledge. He had it to such a degree that, in the end, his listeners were sometimes exhausted by the inextinguishable fireworks of his speech, the inexhaustible fantasy and invention, a kind of prodigal opulence of intellect which astonished his audience.[22]

Was he talking about Herzen, or intuiting Berlin?

Berlin does not identify with Herzen simply because of the rapidity of his tongue. His fundamental principles were the same: history does not follow a libretto, the problems of man have no solution, every society has its own fiber, shortcuts are traps, the cult of abstraction is a sacrificial altar. Man tends to raise temples to his ideas. Temples where human flesh is incinerated. As ideas turn into idols, men become offerings. Many ideas have been exalted: Jus-

---

[22] This description is Pavel Annenkove's, cited by Berlin in "Alexander Herzen," *Russian Thinkers* (London: The Hogarth Press, 1978), p. 189.

tice, Brotherhood, Happiness, Order, Tradition, Progress. Herzen pauses to analyze this god of progress. A form of worship that turns us into a doormat for others to walk all over. What this religion has to offer us is that, after we die, everything will be beautiful. Herzen answers *From the Other Shore*: a remote goal is not a goal; it is a mirage. We cannot become the threshold of the present. "The end of each generation is itself."

There is no libretto, Herzen declares. History has no script that hands out roles, outlines a logical plot, predicts an outcome. History, that autobiography of a madman, is entirely improvised, never failing to amaze: there is no itinerary, no coherence. That is why the goal of life is life itself. Delivering the present up to the promise of a sublime future leads to immolation. That is why we must embrace the ephemeral. Enjoy that which is fleeting. Art and the spark of individual happiness are the only goods within reach. "Why does a singer sing?" Berlin asks, following in the Russian's footsteps. Does he sing because he wants to pay homage to Art? Does he sing in order to anticipate a far more beautiful future song than the one being vocalized? Nonsense. He sings in order to sing. "The purpose of the singer is the song. And the purpose of life is to live it."[23]

Herzen was as adverse to systems as Berlin was. Recipes end up burying the fruit of reality in "the silence of holy stagnation."[24] The world of ideas cannot replace a world of stones, insects, opera, jokes. What is fascinating about Herzen is the fact that his skepticism does not push

---

[23] "Herzen and Bakunin," *ibid*, p. 94.

[24] Alexander Herzen, *Pasado y pensamientos* (Madrid: Tecnos, 1994), p. 171.

him towards passivity, his passion for change does not blind him with illusion. He was an exotic breed: a non-fanatical revolutionary. A revolutionary without a utopia. In the dedication of *From the Other Shore* to his fifteen-year-old son, he asks him not to seek solutions in this book. There are no solutions, he warns him: man has no solution. That which has been resolved is already dead.[25]

If Berlin saw his convictions reflected in Herzen's thinking, he found his existential dilemma in the novelist Turgenev. In his essay on the Russian narrator, Berlin describes the pincer that squeezes the moderate in difficult times. Some dismiss him as a fearful man who defends those in power, while others identity him as an accomplice of the agitators. "Soft as wax," Turgenev sways between the revolutionaries' motives and the traditionalists' reservations. He is horrified by the superstitions and abuses of reactionaries, but he also fears the barbarity of radicalism. He understands older men and wants to make himself understood to the young. And of course, he fails to make a good impression on anybody. As radicalism is inflamed, the field of conciliation is narrowed. Those who resist affiliation on either side of a conflict, those who attempt to dialogue with both extremes are softies, opportunists, cowards; they are indecisive at a time that will not tolerate vacillation.

The indecision of Flaubert's friend is the essential tribulation of the liberal. Or rather, the tribulation of the moderate. A weak man, incapable of committing to his era; a coward who watches a fight to the death while sitting

---

[25] Alexander Herzen, *From the Other Shore* (Oxford: Oxford University Press, 1979), p. 3.

on a fence. The lukewarm, the skittish are paralyzed by doubt. Berlin felt the blame was his. His critics were quick to arrive at the same conclusion. Norman Podhoretz, for example, spoke of his philosophy as a lukewarm tautology that fled from controversy. His moderation, he argues, comes less from the exercise of doubt than from a weakness of character: Berlin, a philosopher without a backbone, couldn't stand the pain of being unpopular. And so Berlin, Christopher Hitchens concludes, was dogged by the need to be found agreeable. He wanted to be valiant, but when he had to make a decision that involved any risk, he would suddenly recall that it was teatime.[26]

Isaiah Berlin's readers are more indebted to the patience of his editor than the perseverance of the writer himself. To Henry Hardy we owe the opportunity to read this timid, wise man who wrote much and published little, who gave extraordinary conferences without preserving any notes from his lessons. The prodigious conversationalist feared the press and thus, accumulated manuscripts in the dusty solitude of his studio. If not for his editor's salvaging, barely a handful of Berlin's texts would remain: his monograph on Marx, his four essays on liberty, and his book on Herder and Vico. The remainder of his works would be lost in the memory of those who attended his conferences, or hidden between the covers of old magazines. Hardy has lent body to a work that otherwise might have vanished into thin air.

---

[26] These critiques come from Norman Podhoretz, "A Dissent on Isaiah Berlin," in *The Norman Podhoretz Reader. A Selection of his Writings from the 1950s through the 1990s* (New York: The Free Press, 2004); and from Christopher Hitchens, "Goodbye to Berlin," in *Unacknowledged Legislation. Writers in the Public Sphere* (London: Verso, 2000).

The collaboration between Hardy and Berlin began in the 1970s, when the historian of ideas was at his prime and the legend of an intellectual *sans oeuvre* had started to take hold. Indeed, Berlin had published very little, and he hadn't the slightest interest in locking himself up to write his great treatise on Romanticism. He was held back by modesty and, perhaps, fear. Berlin always claimed that his talents were limited, and that his prestige was the product of some equivocation. May this error last for a long time, he would conclude. I have had no intellectual agenda. I am a taxi. People flag me down in the middle of the street and I stop, then I go wherever they ask me to go.

Modesty was, perhaps, an inoculation against criticism. The Oxford professor was fearful that the printed word would bear the stamp of his name. He feared that the moment he was subject to the more rigorous examination of reading, his prestige would fall apart. Better the blurred memory of his inimitable voice than the seal of what he rated as mediocrity. Berlin was, in effect, an author in need of an editor. And Henry Hardy was that editor.

As Michael Ignatieff tells it, the two men never became friends. Their manners were quite different. The author was disorderly, capricious, modest; the editor was methodical, obsessive, finicky, even pedantic at times. In professional terms, the momentum was always on the editing side. Hardy stepped on the gas, Berlin slammed on the brakes. The editor wanted to publish everything; the author ceded only a few papers after years of persuasion. If it was Rousseau who said that he had become a philosopher despite himself, it might well be said of Berlin that he became an author very much against his own will. The editor exhumes the remains of a conference, deciphers the scribbles and hieroglyphics found in scattered notes, patiently transcribes old recordings, reconstructs the professor's remarks. The work of Isaiah Berlin is, in a way, the triumph of a stubborn editor over a reluctant author.

There is something miraculous about the publication of Isaiah Berlin's essays. The most amazing of Hardy's achievements was the restoration of the essay on Hamann, the eccentric Prussian thinker who vehemently opposed liberal modernity. Digging through papers and files, Hardy had found an admirable manuscript with long paragraphs dedicated to this writer. Here was a book in the making. But halfway through the final chapter, the argument was suspended with an insert that said: "Why are we here? What is our goal? How can we satisfy..." And at that point, the manuscript was discontinued.

Some time later, Hardy found in the basement of Berlin's home a dusty envelope that said "Hamann." Inside the envelope were several red ribbons. The ribbons were brittle strips incompatible with any existing machine. The technology of these recordings was totally obsolete. He then contacted the National Sound Archive of London, where experts attempted to recover the tapes. They attempted to purchase Agatha Christie's dictaphone, which had recently been put up for auction, but it had already been sold. Finally, the Science Museum located an old, useless dictaphone. The technicians repaired it so that it could play back what seemed to be recordings of a conference about Hamann. The problem of the machine had been resolved. Now the setback was the tapes themselves, which were seriously damaged: time had made them brittle. The strips had to be heated up in an oven in order to soften them. Finally, following considerable suspense, the experts succeeded in transferring the recording onto cassettes. With a trembling hand, Henry Hardy pressed the play button on a conventional tape recorder. From the machine, through a dense curtain of sound, the galloping voice of Berlin emerged. After listening for a while, he was finally able to hear him say the words: "Why are we here? What is our goal? How can we satisfy –how can we allay the spiritual agony of those who will not rest unless they obtain true answers to these questions?" And after that, he heard him continue until the chapter had been completed, then go on to compose the next until reaching the conclusions of the essay. The book on Hamann was born.

Through portraying the contradictory nature of our ideals, Berlin was able to understand how to embrace his own ambiguities. A liberal with a tragic air, he was far from market dogmatism and a staunch defender of his aspiration to fit in. Some have read his defense of negative liberty as praise for the minimal state, a defense of economic competition where the government is simply a watchdog. Berlin always considered himself a leftist liberal. He was convinced that liberty could not flourish in a society marked by ignorance and poverty. That is why he admired Roosevelt's New Deal as a policy that, in his inhospitable world, had found a way to reconcile liberty and equality.

Belonging was, to him, a continual thirst. Having been torn from his native land as a small child, he felt the need to form part of a community. In this sense, Berlin's liberalism does not declare itself to be a rival of community. He understood the national appetite. If there is a nationalism that bites, there is also a nationalism that blankets. Opposite that nationalism of tight jaws, resentful memories and quarrelsome pride, there is also a gentler nationalism that warms. This is a tranquil sort of nationalism, one that allows a man to feel at home among his own kind. Berlin found Herder to be a seeker of this sense of belonging. "He believed that just as people need to eat and drink, to have security and freedom of movement, so too they need to belong to a group. Deprived of this, they felt cut off, lonely diminished, unhappy."[27] Herder showed that nationalism could be non-political, non-aggressive. The cosmopolitanism of liberals or socialists was to him an empty endeavor that ignored the most profound desires of mankind. That is why he was a Zionist. He wanted the Jews to have a country, a home. He knew that nationalism could be stupid or criminal, but he also honored the warmth of community: its memories, celebrations, and flavors.[28]

Berlinean nationalism seems more like a state of mind than an intellectual conviction. He abhorred the organicist notions that transform the individual into an insignificant, disposable cell; he ridiculed the stubbornness of one who continues on a road just because it is his, even if it leads off a cliff; he feared the violence of nationalist resentment. He would say as much: nationalism is a dis-

---

[27] "Two Concepts of Nationalism: An interview with Isaiah Berlin," by Nathan Gardels, *The New York Review of Books*, vol. 38 no. 19 (21 November 1991).

[28] Regarding Berlin's nationalism and Zionism, read Buruma's essay "The Last Englishman...", *cit.*, and "The Crooked Timber of Nationalism," by Avishai Margalit, compiled in Ronald Dworkin, Mark Lila, and Robert B. Silvers, *The Legacy of Isiaiah Berlin* (New York: The New York Review of Books, 2001).

ease, an infected wound. And even so, he understood the value of belonging.

He belonged, as chance would have it, to a specific family. To a nation with its rainy weather, fables, dinner parties and pastries. Like the reactionary he had studied, he would say that man as such, in the abstract, is a non-existent animal; those talking creatures who live on the planet Earth are Germans, Russians, Italians, Mexicans. Thereby his suspicions regarding the universal mold of the encyclopedists. He quoted that paragraph where Montesquieu agreed with Moctezuma, who argued that the religion of the Spaniards was good for them, while the Aztec religion was good for his own people. Regarding liberalism, Berlin eventually said that being a European plant, it would be difficult to sow in other climates. I suspect, he said, that there are few liberals in Korea, and I doubt that there is liberalism in Latin America. "I think liberalism is essentially the belief of people who have lived on the same soil for a long time in comparative peace with each other. An English invention."[29]

In one of the few voyages he made outside his world, he confronted a culture that turned out to be quite disturbing to him. In early 1945, Berlin caught a nasty bug: nothing too serious. He was working at the British Embassy in Washington and one of his colleagues, the son-in-law of Dwight Morrow, the former U.S. Ambassador to Mexico, invited him to Cuernavaca to get some rest and recover from his illness. The climate and tranquility would do him good. Thus, Berlin spent ten days at Casa

[29] The quote comes from "Isaiah Berlin in Conversation with Steven Lukes," *Salmagundi,* no. 120 (Autumn 1998).

Mañana in Cuernavaca and a day or two in Mexico City. The letters gathered by Henry Hardy tell us of his impressions. There are no letters or postcards dated in Mexico, but there are a few references to his visit in later missives. As therapy, the solar treatment in Cuernavaca was effective: upon returning to Washington, Isaiah commented to his parents that he was in perfect health. His impression of Mexico, however, is a blend of fascination and horror, of anthropological curiosity and physical repulsion. Berlin felt very pleased at having the opportunity to visit Mexico, but he made it very clear that he had no interest whatsoever in going back. Mexico was a strange, savage, coarse, and reserved sort of country. Mexico was a land "full of cruelty and a kind of barbaric imagination" to which Berlin hoped never to return. Twelve days had been more than enough. His impressions regarding Mexicans are contradictory: on the one hand, he saw intense, profound temperaments, animated by a rich inner life. On the other, he recalls them as dark, ferocious characters dominated by superstition and barbarism.

> The soil in Mexico is obviously very rich and rank and capable of the most luxuriant vegetation, but the looks on people's faces rather terrified me. I could respect them and admire them, but I do not think ever feel comfortable among them.

The professor saw Mexico as a country with botanical exuberance and social savagery that could hardly form part of liberal civilization. Apparently, English flora could not be transplanted just anywhere. In order to become acclimated, liberty needed to find a culture of tolerance and a history of peace. Liberalism for the rich man. Christopher Hitchens made the leap: liberalism for those who don't need it.[30]

At some point Isaiah Berlin wrote that his one true passion was music. His public life hung on his gaze, but his private life followed the labyrinths of his ear. This is clearly revealed in his letters: he enjoyed the spoils of a library, rejoiced in conversation, was disquieted by politics. But he lived to track down concerts, to listen to the scores of Bach, the quartets of Beethoven, the sonatas of Schubert, the symphonies of Mozart. He lived to attend the festival at Salzburg, to meet Toscanini, to witness a new staging of *Nabucco*, and to hear the philharmonic of Vienna or the piano of Arthur Schnabel. Berlin would cross half of Europe to hear a concert. Of all his hobbies, there was none that filled him with as much enjoyment as being the director of the London Opera at Covent Garden. Isaiah Berlin attended every performance. He put together the season's repertoire. He scouted for directors, hired the singers he admired, wrote the program notes. Upon describing Verdi in one of his essays, he was naming his own sensitivity:

> He was the last master to paint with positive, clear, primary colours, to give direct expression to the eternal, major human emotions: love and hate, jealousy and fear, indignation and passion; grief, fury, mockery, cruelty, irony, fanaticism, faith, the passions that all men know. After him, this is much more rare.[31]

---

[30] Christopher Hitchens, "Goodbye to Berlin," *cit.*, p. 162.

[31] From "The '*Naïveté*' of Verdi," in *Against the Current* (Princeton, New Jersey: Princeton University Press, 1979), p. 294.

A few years before his death, Isaiah Berlin imagined his funeral like a concerto: Alfred Brendel playing a Schubert sonata. And so it was. On January 14, 1998, during a memorial service held at the Hampstead synagogue in London, Alfred Brendel played the Sonata in A Minor by Schubert. The soft melancholy of its initial phrases is suddenly swept away by a storm. Tragedy there, among the melodiousness. Brendel was one of Berlin's last great friends. They were joined, naturally, by their love for music. And also by a perfect trio of aversions: noise, cigarette smoke, and fanatics.

During the same ceremony, Bernard Williams, one of the men closest to Isaiah Berlin, said that the image that would remind him most of his friend would not be that of his brilliant speech with an accent that was so unique, so much his own. I will remember him listening to his music, he said. Concentrating on the melody, moving along lightly. Lost somewhere beyond words, arguments, or history.

Enamoured Syllables

To be has no opposite.
Antonio Machado

Thought is based on uprooting. To fence with words, Octavio Paz said, is "to pull one's being up out of primordial chaos,"[1] a fissure opened in the Western world by the blade of a poet born in Elea over twenty-five centuries ago.

Parmenides narrates his voyage into the Light mounted on a fanciful chariot and escorted by solar damsels. After opening the gates of night and day with gentle words, he encounters an unnamed goddess. The divinity benevolently welcomes the poet and reveals to him the "beautifully circular" core of Truth.

> Come now, I will tell thee –and do thou hearken to my saying and carry it away– the only two ways of search that can be thought of. The first, namely, that *It is*, and that it is impossible for anything not to be, is the way of conviction, for truth is its companion.

---

[1] Octavio Paz, *El arco y la lira, Obras completas*, vol. I (Mexico: Fondo de Cultura Económica, 1995), p. 116.

That which exists *is*, and that which does not deserves no words. Thereby the sharp knife of Parmenides, the blade of disjunction that continues to tear us apart. Man is not dust; water does not burn; lightness does not oppress us. Reality is an imperturbable entity. Many of Parmenides' contemporaries thought he was a cretin: just by opening one's eyes, the exuberance of objects is plain to see; the incessant shifting of life, the presence of ambiguity, the irony of bodies. Reality, Parmenides would respond, is something we observe not with the retina, but with the closed eyelids of intelligence. Imagination is banned. That which is nothing, comes from nothingness.

Whereas according to Rousseau, the decline of our civilization began with property, Octavio Paz felt our vulnerability was created by definition. Our sorrows did not begin the moment someone said, "this is mine," but the moment someone said: "this is this, and cannot be that." Two human sins: taking possession of Nature (something that belongs to all) and imprisoning the variable meaning of things. This fence of being, this wall that divides the world into two halves, this logical prison that our thought cannot break free of is the hearth of the Western world. Therein lies our uprootedness: words are left in pieces, and we are divided along with them.

Everything belonged to everyone
Everyone was all
There was only a vast, one-sided word
A word like the sun
One fine day it was broken into tiny pieces
These are the words of the language we spoke

Fragments never to be joined
Broken mirrors in which the world could see itself destroyed

Words tear, but they also bind. The poet's task is to recreate the original brotherhood of meaning. Poetic images breach walls and say the unspeakable. Feathers become stones. "The universe is no longer a vast warehouse of heterogeneous things. Stars, shoes, tears, locomotives, weeping willows, women, and dictionaries are all one great family, all is interconnected and continually transformed, the same blood runs through all forms, and man can finally become what he desires: himself."[2] At the root of poetry is found the communion between man and the world, between plants and volcanoes. When he received the Nobel Prize in Stockholm, Paz recalled a night outdoors when he was able to perceive the correspondence between celestial bodies and insects:

The heavens are great
and worlds are sown above.
Imperturbable,
the cricket auger
persists in all that night.

The poem as a field for reconciliation. An instantaneous pact between opposing forces, this poem finds a hidden affinity between the distant realities of cricket and cosmos. Writing recreates a cosmic fraternity that has been mutilated by logic. Both an awareness of contradiction

[2] *Ibid.*, vol. 1, p. 126.

and a desire for reconciliation manifested themselves in Paz very early on, even as a boy living in the Mexico City neighborhood of Mixcoac. He told Julio Scherer that his childhood home was:

> ...the stage for a struggle between generations. My grandfather –a liberal journalist and writer– fought against the French intervention and later supported Porfirio Díaz. Something he would repent at the end of his days. My father used to say that my grandfather didn't understand the Mexican Revolution, and my grandfather would reply that the Revolution had substituted the dictatorship of one, the strongman Díaz, for the anarchic dictatorship of many: bosses and local chieftains who, back then, would kill each other for power.

My grandfather, drinking his coffee,
would tell me about Juárez and Porfirio,
the Zouaves and the Plateado bandits.
And the tablecloth smelled of gunpowder.

My father, while raising his glass,
would tell me of Zapata and Villa,
Soto and Gama and the Flores Magóns.
And the tablecloth smelled of gunpowder.

I would remain silent:
whom could I speak of?

The grandfather's coffee challenges the father's alcohol. These liquids confront each other: they clash, intermingle, drown each other out. They would later be blended together on the palate of Octavio Paz Lozano. Liberalism has no need to slay the ancestral community; being attached to the earth does not require the annihilation of legality. From then on, Paz discarded confrontation as an option: not this *or* that, but rather this *with* that. "My grandfather was right, but what my father said was also true."[3] Out of these candescent arguments sprang the mark of Pazian literature: the reconciliation of opposites. Paz knew that even in the most starkly contrasted voices, there was deep kinship. His work was an extension of those breakfast conversations: dialogues between John Donne and Apollinaire; between the serpents of the goddess Coatlicue and the dancing colors of Miró; between Pessoa and his heteronyms; between all three stances of surrealism; between Quevedo, Machado, and Ortega y Gasset; between Sor Juana and Alfonso Reyes; between the tastes and smells of India, its myths and forms; between Chinese poetry, *fin de siècle* dissidents, and colonial inquisitors; between eroticism and democracy. Dialogues that shed light on a civilization: Octavio Paz's civilization.

Conversations marked by a desire to transcend contradiction. The tablecloth in Mixcoac, cleaving into Parmenides' knife. The tablecloth as a bridge that drives away all classifications and disjunctions. As Manuel Ulacia rightly observed, in Octavio Paz's poetry and essays, time and time again these couplings of opposites take place.[4]

---

[3] "Suma y sigue" (Conversation with Julio Scherer), *OC* vol. 8, p. 366.

[4] See "La conciliación de los contrarios" in Adolfo Castañón, Ramón Xirau *et al.*, *Octavio Paz en sus "Obras completas"* (Mexico: Conaculta and Fondo de Cultura Económica, 1994), and his complete study *El árbol milenario. Un recorrido por la obra de Octavio Paz* (Barcelona: Círculo de Lectores, 1999).

The rhythmic tapping that sustains his thought consists of estranged columns standing side by side: solitude and communion, union and separation, arrow and target, rupture and reconciliation, modernity and tradition, confluences and divergences, immobility and dance. The key was to be found outside the Western world. Taoist philosopher Chuang-Tzu, for example, who said:

> If there is no other that is not me, neither can I exist. But if there is no me, nothing can be known, said, or thought [...] In truth, all beings are *Others*, and all beings are themselves [...] The Other knows of himself, but depends himself as well on the Other [...] To adopt affirmation is to adopt negation.[5]

In *White*, a poem of diverse voices that travels through the territories of love, words, and knowledge, a poem Paz considered to be one of his most complex and ambitious works, we find these lines that synthesize his effort to find the missing half, the negated half of man.

> No and Yes
> together
> two syllables in love[6]

Imagination is an invisible character that casts a spell over the enamored duo. In Paz's work, imagination is not the "madwoman of the house," as Saint Teresa would nickname her, but rather the supreme exercise of intelligence.

---

[5] "Nosotros: los otros," *OC* vol. 10, p. 33.

[6] *The Collected Poems of Octavio Paz,* trans. Eliot Weinberger (San Francisco: New Directions, 1990), p. 328.

To be able to associate seemingly distant entities is to get at the truth of the matter. "Poetry is coming into being," he wrote in *The Bow and the Lyre*. Not the being of appearances or logic, but the being of something even more human: words.

> The means of operation in poetic thought is imagination, and this consists, essentially, of the faculty of relating contrary or dissimilar elements. All poetic forms and all figures of language possess a common characteristic: they seek, and frequently find, hidden similarities between different objects. In very rare cases, they bring opposites together. Comparisons, analogies, metaphors, metonyms, and other resources of poetry: all of these tend to produce images in which a pact is made between this and that, one and the other, many and one.

To write is to seek. To pursue the center of the moment, deducing the world from its river. To salvage, to petrify what time dissolves. "Writing is the incessant interrogation by many signs of one sign: man; and by this sign of many signs: language." A passion for the passion for knowledge, no less, a passion for knowledge that is none other than the love for words. This was why Pere Gimferrer called him a "poet of thought." A poet in the same family as John Donne, Quevedo, Wordsworth, T.S. Eliot, or Valery.[7] The Catalonian poet knew the rigors of Paz's poetic imagination. A poem is a form of knowledge. A letter addressed to Gimferrer written by the Mexican poet on a typical day in 1967 serves as an example of these demands.

---

[7] "Poesía del pensamiento," *Vuelta* (Mexico: May 1998).

> Dear Gimferrer: words are to be doubted. Or you may trust in them, but do not try to guide or subdue them. Struggle with language. Continue onward with the exploration and explosion that began in *The Sea that Burns*. Today, reading in a newspaper an article about some film or other, I stumbled upon this phrase: man is not a bird. And I thought: saying man is not a bird is akin to saying something that should go unsaid, because it is already known. But to say that man is a bird is a cliché. So [...] then the poet must find the *other* word, the unsaid word that the ellipses after "so" designate as silence. Struggle, therefore, with silence.

In another letter, his reading of his friend continues:

> I believe you must follow the same path you have already started out on and bring this experience to its conclusion. A word of advice, if I may? Complete it as rigorously as possible, because otherwise it won't be an experience, but a blunder. I like the new poems you have sent me more than the previous ones, but they do not substantially alter my first impression. I repeat: it isn't a question of theme, but of rigor. In the first place: vocabulary. I would suppress many adjectives that are obvious or predictable. One example: the *subtle* stride of the dwarf, the *floral* whisper of the gulfweed, etc. I would also suppress explanatory phrases: the voice of sirens that seems to emerge from our own chest. Isn't there a more "economic" way of saying this? You hope, I imagine, to *show* rather than to *evoke*, but often your poems are not snapshots, but rather evocations: you don't let things speak for themselves, you intervene.[8]

---

[8] Octavio Paz, *Memorias y palabras. Cartas a Pere Gimferrer, 1966-1977* (Barcelona: Seix Barral, 1999).

The rigors of imagination.

Paz's work is a prolonged, convincing allegation that defends the rights of poetry. Enrico Mario Santí put it well: poetry frames his entire work; not just making poetry or thinking about it but, above all, thinking *from* poetry.[9]

> Between doing and seeing
> action or contemplation
> I chose the act of words:
> making them, inhabiting them,
> lending eyes to language.

The naked declaration of his vocation: to make works, to inhabit words. The inhabitant of language listens to the world poetically; thus, he names it. Poetry in Paz is not a fantasy: it is a contemplation that navigates between philosophy and history. Being without one or the other is, like philosophy, contemplation, and like history, a clamp that grips what is concrete. Poetic discourse meets man halfway, his art, literature, habits, and power. Paz's critical passion also comes to embrace political issues. Giving a speech after having received the Alexis de Tocqueville prize in 1989, Paz said:

> Since my adolescence I have written poems, and I have never stopped writing them. I always wanted to be a poet, nothing

[9] "Los derechos de la poesía," in Adolfo Castañón, Ramón Xirau *et al.*, *Octavio Paz en sus "Obras completas," op. cit.*

> more. In my books, I took it upon myself to serve poetry, to justify and defend it, to explain it to others and myself. I soon discovered that the defense of poetry, despised in our century, was inseparable from the defense of freedom. Thereby my passionate interest in the political and social issues that have agitated our time.[10]

Poetry getting mixed up in issues of sovereignty. There has been no condemnation of this interference more energetic than that of Plato, who was a poet himself. Plato chose to expel poetry from the perfect city, petrified by reason. Poetry as a rival of truth, unity, order. Inventing worlds for words, breaking away from meaning, remembering that which has lost its name and designating that which does not exist is to tear apart the impenetrable sculpture of utopia. Heretical, drunken, subversive, and melancholy, poetry cannot claim jurisdiction over serious matters of State. The poet might be able to liven up the symposium, but never cast judgment on the members of parliament. The struggle between two forms of words –philosophical and poetic– is resolved in Plato by the execution of poetry. And so, as María Zambrano says, the random, illegal life of poetry spreads: its curse.[11]

Paz did not attempt to hide behind the vocabulary of a specialist in order to talk about history or politics. "I prefer to speak of Marcel Duchamp or Juan Ramón Jiménez than Locke or Montesquieu. Political philosophy has always interested me, but I have never attempted nor will

[10] "Poesía, mito, revolución," in *OC* vol. 1, p. 522.

[11] María Zambrano, *Filosofía y poesía* (Madrid: Fondo de Cultura Economica, 1993), pp. 13-14.

I attempt to write a book about justice, freedom, or the art of government."[12] Lacking any theoretical pretensions, his political reflections are reflexes, lucid and profound writings of a witness to events. Opinions. The strength of his words is derived from impotence. "A writer's word is forceful because it springs from a situation lacking in force. He doesn't speak from the National Palace, the popular tribune, or the offices of the Central Committee: he speaks from his room."[13] In a century intoxicated by ideologies –walled in, self-satisfied beliefs– Octavio Paz brandishes the needle of criticism. Critique "is our only defense against the monologue of the Strongman and the cries of the Masses, twin distortions that extirpate the *other*."

To write poetry, or to defend it, demands that one become involved in politics or, in other words, the defense of freedom. But what exactly is freedom, according to Octavio Paz? Time and time again in his essays, he resists the capsule of definition. Honing the meaning of the word freedom would enslave it; that is why he says it is not about a concept, but an act. Or rather, a gamble. Free is the man who says "no," the one who turns around and refuses to continue along the same path. We invent freedom by exercising it. Like Camus, Paz affirms that merely to exist is rebellious. That is why this poet does not follow the lead of technical experts who attempt to reduce lib-

[12] "La democracia: Lo absoluto y lo relativo," *OC* vol. 9, p. 473.

[13] "El escritor y el poder," *OC* vol. 8, p. 549. "Where do you write from, the center, the left, from where?" Braulio Peralta asks him. Paz answers: "From my room, from my solitude, from myself. Never from others." Braulio Peralta, *El poeta en su tierra. Diálogos con Octavio Paz* (Mexico: Raya en el Agua, 1999).

erty to a shield that protects us from the State. The modern freedom of Benjamin Constant or the negative freedom of Isaiah Berlin can turn into a chamber that traps us within ourselves. That is why, unlike these engineers, Paz desires a freedom with eyes wide open. A dangerous, self-absorbed freedom, imprisoned by its own solitude. Miserable is the man who doesn't succeed in detaching himself from himself: "a rotten idol." Freedom is a feat of the imagination.

> Freedom is wings,
> it is wind between the sheets, detained
> by a mere flower; and the dream
> in which we are our dream;
> it is biting into the forbidden orange,
> opening that old condemned door
> and untying the prisoner:
> that stone is now bread,
> these white papers are seagulls,
> the sheets are birds
> and your fingers, birds: everything flies.

At age twenty-one, Octavio Paz wrote that "to be is to limit oneself, to acquire an outline."[14] Freedom, the existence of man itself, demands the presence of another. The other is at the heart of one's self. This is the key to *The Labyrinth of Solitude* and the conclusion of *PostScript*: otherness is what constitutes us. "We sought ourselves and found others." He says this very clearly when writ-

---

[14] "Vigilias: diario de un soñador," *OC* vol. 8, p. 147.

ing about the erotic poetry of Luis Cernuda: to be is to desire. "Every time we love, we lose ourselves: we become another. Love does not fulfill one's self, it opens up the possibility for the 'I' to change, to be converted. In love, it is not the 'I' but the person who is fulfilled: the desire to be another. The desire to be."[15] To be is to overflow.

Liberalism might be the most hospitable thing in the world, but it leaves all of our questions about the origin and meaning of life unanswered. In Paz, we find a moderate, that is to say, a Tocquevillean love for liberal democracy. What he loves about it is the civility of its coexistence, its generosity, the presence of criticism. But he also knows that the answers to the core riddles of our existence are not to be found in democratic venues. Modern democracies ignore the Other and tend toward conformity, toward "smiles of idiotic satisfaction."

> [Liberalism] founded liberty on the sole foundation capable of sustaining it: the autonomy of awareness and the recognition of the autonomy of alien awareness. It was admirable and also terrible: it locked us into a solipsism, it broke the bridge that joined the I to the You and then both of these to the third person: the Other, the Others. Between liberty and fraternity there is no contradiction, there is only distance –a distance that liberalism has not been able to annul.

It has failed to close the gap because it has not completed its immersion in the Other. Therefore liberalism, according to Paz, is not bound to itself.

---

[15] "Luis Cernuda," *OC* vol. 3, p. 253.

In "Sunstone," Octavio Paz describes this need to find the Other:

> (...) in order to be I must be another,
> leave myself, search for myself
> in the others, the others that don't exist
> if I don't exist, the others that give me
> total existence, I am not,
> there is no I, we are always us,
> life is other, always there,
> further off, beyond you and
> beyond me, always on the horizon,
> life which unlives us and makes us strangers,
> that invents our face and wears it away (...)[16]

In his argument about the shortcomings of liberalism, Octavio Paz does not realize that one of the most important contributions of liberalism is precisely the set of questions that are no longer asked. The liberal mind focuses on the orbit of politics, seeking only that man become his own master. He knows that by accepting the fact that power won't guide him through the mystery of life, he will be spared its threats. Liberalism is not, and does not intend to be, a religion; it is a strategy. And yet this is not its weakness, as Paz would claim, but rather its greatness.

Paz did not proclaim himself a liberal. The hat was too tight for him. He simply felt akin to liberalism: "My most true and profound affinities lie with liberal heritage."[17] As

---

[16] *The Collected Poems of Octavio Paz,* trans. Eliot Weinberger, pp. 30-31.

[17] "Pequeña crónica de grandes días," in *OC* vol. 9, p. 471.

Yvon Grenier has highlighted, the moderate word *affinity* is crucial in this relationship of trust. Affinity: proximity, similarity; not belonging. More than liberalism, Paz is moved by an idea that remains nameless. It might be called *fraternism* in the near future. A policy centered on fraternity, the forgotten corner of the French triangle. A poem, let us recall, captures cosmic fraternity: the brotherhood of cricket and stars. This is the other voice that the new political philosophy must hear. "The word *fraternity* is no less precious than the word *liberty*: it is the bread of men, the bread they break."

> As I see it, the main word of the triad (liberty, equality, fraternity) is *fraternity*. In it are intertwined the other two. Liberty can exist without equality, and equality without liberty. The former, in isolation, deepens inequalities and provokes tyrannies; the latter oppresses liberty and in the end, annihilates it. Fraternity is the link that communicates them, the virtue that humanizes and harmonizes them. Its other name is solidarity, living heritage of Christianity, modern version of ancient charity. A virtue that neither the Greeks nor the Romans knew, enamored of liberty but ignorant of true compassion. Given the natural differences between men, equality is an ethical aspiration that cannot be fulfilled without recurring to despotism or the action of fraternity. Likewise, my liberty is fatally confronted with the liberty of the Other and procures its annulment. The only bridge that can reconcile these two enemy sisters –a bridge made of intertwined arms– is fraternity. Over this humble and simple evidence can be founded a new political philosophy in days to come. Only fraternity can dissipate the circular nightmare of the market. I warn that I am but imagining, or, to be more precise, catching a

> glimpse of this thought. I see it as the heir of the dual tradition of modernity: liberalism and socialism. I don't believe that they should be repeated, but rather transcended. That would be a true renovation.[18]

The poet discovers through his imagination all that liberalism represses, all that liberalism has forgotten. He always regarded with mistrust, for example, the impersonal and inflexible cycle of the market. A blind, deaf monster that knows no courage. Thus the romantic condemns profit, the vice of commerce that opposes us like beasts. From "Between the flower and the stone," his first attempt at "inserting poetry into history," Paz denounces the cruelties of this cold machinery.

> Money and its wheel,
> money and its many gaps,
> money and its herd of specters.

"Knowing how to tell," Paz would write on another occasion, "is not knowing how to sing." That is why the search for liberty cannot be isolated from the search for communion. If poetic imagination is capable of infatuating the syllable that affirms with the one that denies, the same potential should reconcile enemy doctrines. An error, as Pascal would say, is not contrary to the truth; it is having forgotten the opposite truth. Paz played upon strings contrary to politics: the reasons behind liberty and community traditions, individual rights and the embrace

---

[18] "La otra voz," in *OC* vol. 1, p. 586.

of brotherhood. No wonder he would find in Cornelius Castoriadis the key to philosophical renewal, given that there, imagination has a constitutive character. "The soul," Castoriadis reminds Aristotle, "never thinks without ghosts." The crisis of our civilization is the depletion of these ghosts, the hollowing out of meaning, dry imagination, arrogant conformity. The democracy Castoriadis defended was not the empty ritual of elections, but the living civilization of queries, the house of open doors.

Born eight years after Octavio Paz, far away from Mixcoac, Castoriadis tried to salvage the libertarian ideal of socialism. A man with a shaven head, juicy smile and radiant complexion, Castoriadis boiled over with intelligence. Nothing can supplant, he said, the enjoyment of a discussion, wine, music, and a good joke. From his readings of Marx and his practice as a psychoanalyst, from his love for ancient Greece and his close observation of striking miners, from his poetic sensitivity and his practice as an economist came a democratic idea that goes far beyond any competition between parties. Democracy makes sense when it truly cultivates a society of autonomous men, of men capable of choosing their paths. A regime in which all questions can be asked.

It is up to the poet to reanimate political philosophy in order to encounter a new world of meanings in which ideas lose their thorny shrouds. Along these same lines we find the proposal of Leszek Kolakowski, who wrote a manual for conservatives, liberals, and socialists alike that combats precisely that old philosophy of mutually exclusive philosophies. The Polish philosopher proposed as a motto for his own International a phrase he once heard on a bus in Warsaw: "Move ahead backwards, please." Kolakowski argued that the waters of these rivers did not necessarily have to flow in different beds. They could just as easily pour their waters out into the same bowl. A conservative knows that improvements are costly, that every reform has its cost; he doubts that the suppression of traditions will make us any happier, and he mistrusts utopias. He abominates, above all, those who attempt to use the machinery of the State to set us on the path to paradise. A liberal demands that the State guarantee our freedom, not that it ensure our happiness. Finally, a socialist categorically denies that inequality is a hopeless curse. That perfection is unattainable doesn't mean that nothing can be done to diminish oppression.[19] Confronted by the tyranny of the O, we find the utopian Y. The right not to choose. That's how Paz puts it in a poem:

to choose

is to err

Paz chose not to choose: he was a romantic, a liberal, a conservative, a socialist, a libertarian. All at once. He defended freedom and representative democracy while at the same time rejecting the idolatry of reason and progress. He valued the flow of tradition, he feared the crash of revolution, and he aspired to a fraternal world. It corresponds to the imagination to find that conciliatory bridge, a bond of convergence for the two great modern

[19] Leszek Kolakowski, *Modernity on Endless Trial* (Chicago, Illinois: The University of Chicago Press, 1990).

traditions: liberalism and socialism. True enough: of the roundtable needed to reach this pact, Paz tells us very little. The poet names, gleans, and shows; he doesn't hand out recipes. He seeks out new waters.

Politics Were Not the Passion of Octavio Paz, Poet.

> The history of modern literature from the German and English Romantics to our time is that of a long, ill-fated passion for politics. From Coleridge to Mayakovsky, the Revolution has been the great Goddess, the eternal Beloved and grand Whore of poets and novelists. Politics filled Malraux's brain with smoke, poisoned the insomnias of César Vallejo, killed García Lorca, abandoned old Machado in a village of the Pyrenees, locked Pound up in an insane asylum, dishonored Neruda and Aragón, made a fool of Sartre and proved Breton right, albeit too late.[20]

Politics is felt, thus, as a curse. A curse that debases intelligence and riddles the apples of our eyes with worms. Paz was never overly enthusiastic about politics. He was interested, certainly –or rather, concerned. He knew that no matter how damned, politics cannot be ignored: to ignore them would be worse than spitting into the wind.

The concept of evil underlies all of his political meditations. "Evil: an anonymous somebody." Out of that conviction, he became a liberal who saw power as a threat, never as a bridge to redemption. His was a liberalism that, at some point, began to flirt with anarchy: "we should

---

[20] See the essay by Yvon Grenier, *Del arte a la política. Octavio Paz y la búsqueda de la libertad* (Mexico: Fondo de Cultura Económica, 2004).

burn all of the chairs and thrones," he came to write, in the throes of Zapatismo. One's guard can never be let down before the cruel, seductive demon of power. Octavio Paz's lengthy reflection about history and politics unfolds into just two questions. "Are we evil? Or is evil on the outside, and we are its instrument, its tool?" No, Paz answers. Evil lies within: at the core of our conscience, at the very root of freedom. "This is the only lesson I can derive from a long and sinuous itinerary: to struggle against evil is to struggle against ourselves. And that is the meaning of history."[21] Therefore, unlike many of the most brilliant men of his century, he never approached politics as one would seek God, or intend to finally encounter good under the misguided belief that the essential answers can be found in politics.

Of course, a liberalism that is constantly *en garde* against evil cannot stand alone, because no words stand alone in Paz's work. Every utterance in his language is an invitation to mate with its opposite. To state that Octavio Paz was liberal is a cliché. He was obviously a liberal: he stubbornly defended the autonomy of the individual, he denounced despotism on all sides, he criticized absolutes, he was a militant of doubt. But he was also a liberal who adopted many critiques of liberalism as his own, viewing it as a rough sketch that was at the same time both admirable and *terrible*.

There is no polished political doctrine to be found in the works of Paz. But there is, beyond a doubt, a dense and coherent meditation on the randomness of history,

---

[21] "*Itinerario,* " in *OC* vol. 9, p. 66.

the traps of ideology, and the possibility of coexistence. It would be worthwhile to focus on his contributions toward comprehending Mexican change. The first steps toward Mexican democracy shed new light on Paz's political writings. Reading today his notes about the nature of bureaucracy, the vices of the Institutional Revolutionary Party (PRI), the intellectual shortcomings of the National Action Party (PAN), the leeches of the left, the drool of demagoguery, and the complex and demanding texture of democratic pluralism is to concede that Gonzalo Rojas was right when he said on that sad day, April 19, 1998: "A dead man speaks to us still."

No one understood as Octavio Paz did the machinery of post-revolutionary power in Mexico, no one anticipated the roads of democratization, or foretold with such clarity the rhythm of change and acidity of future threats. With far greater lucidity than the university professors, the poet who mocked politology sensed the peculiarities of PRI domination, anticipated and demanded its authentic change, foretold democratic dearth. Reading Paz, we find ourselves in the present.

Rethinking the present implies recovering Paz's critical gaze. "We have to learn in order to become air, to dream freely." *Dream freely*. These are the words from which *Posdata* flows. Also derived from there is the title of an anthology of political writings by Octavio Paz prepared by Yvon Grenier. "If politics are a dimension of history, political and moral criticism are as well. We must confront the Mexico of the Main Square, of Tlaltelolco and the Museum of Anthropology not with another image –all images suffer from a fatal tendency toward petrification– but with criticism: *the acid that dissolves images.*" A critique can do battle against stagnant dreams, striking a sable blow against the cobwebs of ideology. This is where Paz's validity stems from, the enemy of ideology in a century of ideological drunkenness.

Paz cultivated the art of discernment: when faced by many things, he saw every single one. That is why he never sympathized with simplifiers. Social truths always become comedies of errors. Paz always countered the caricature of Mexico's post-revolutionary regime as a dictatorship akin to those of South America, or a close cousin of the one-party systems in Eastern Europe, with reasons. Anyone who has lived under a dictatorship will realize that there was no such thing in Mexico. Post-revolutionary politics may not have been democratic by any means, but neither can they be considered a facsimile of Francoism. Paz may have been a critic of power, but first and foremost he was a critic. For him, intelligence always came before willpower. In order to oppose the PRI political regime (a peculiar form of bureaucratic domination, patrimonialist and authoritarian) the first order of business was to understand it without the deformations of idealogues, who accommodate everything according to prejudice. They believe that the more disqualifications you launch at the body of your adversary, the stronger you become. But they are weakened, Paz argued, because they deceive themselves by abdicating critical intelligence. Paz sought comprehension, above all. "I refuse to succumb to the over-simplifications that are in vogue in order to criticize the PRI."

The peculiarities of the Mexican ogre enabled him

to anticipate the route of democratization. It would not be revolution, but reform that would end this regime of emergence inaugurated by Calles. A reform, Paz had anticipated since *Postdata*, that would not render fruit immediately. The path of reformism would be slow and hazardous. After the regime, many players would resist handing over their privileges; the opposition was riddled with weaknesses. Their Jacobin fascination with rupture did not dazzle him. He believed that the political regime should and could proceed towards its democratic transformation. What stood in the way of this transition was the "unnatural prolongation of the political monopoly" of the PRI and the immaturity of its adversaries.

This last point seems especially relevant to me. As the enemy of essentialism in any shape or form, he did not arrive at the conclusion that a democratizing energy had been deposited in some historically privileged subject. The opposition was not the exclusive carrier of the democratic banner, nor was Civil Society the chosen mother of democracy. The problem was the absence of democrats. "The PRI ought to attend a school for democracy," Paz would say. And then he would immediately add, "The opposition parties also ought to enroll there." Many considered this to be a parsimonious reaction to the drumbeat of democratization. And perhaps they have a point: having seen the adversaries of the PRI, Paz was in no rush to have them as political enemies. In the National Action Party (PAN) he saw a prudish, provincial party. Over the years, his mistrust was ameliorated somewhat, but he continued to believe that the right was not interested in ideas, that debates gave them a headache. They might grow and win elections, but they had no project for Mexico. In the groups of former PRI members and former communists who would later consolidate as the PRD he saw the worst sort of left rear its ugly head: demagogy, populism, state worship, authoritarianism. If the ardent democratic convictions of the neo-Cardenists are sincere, Paz wrote, then they are very recent.

It never fails to amaze that the political writer most invoked by Paz in his collected political writings was Karl Marx. The title of his first book has a Marxist air: *The Root of Man*. To be radical is to get at the root of the matter. Paz saw his erotic poetry as a naturally revolutionary act. The great liberal authors hardly make an appearance among these pages. Benjamin Constant pops up in an epigraph and then disappears, Locke is summoned three times, Isaiah Berlin, never. In contrast, Marx is cited on twenty-nine occasions. The author of *The Philanthropic Ogre* wanted to argue with the left. As for the right, there was nothing to say. Thereby Paz's frustration with the absence of replica. What exasperated him was the left's renunciation of criticism: "The great failure of the left –its tragedy– is that time and time again, above all in the 20th century, it has forgotten its original vocation, its birthmark: criticism. It has sold out its heritage for that plate of lentils known as a closed system, an ideology."[22]

The thread of Paz's political thought is tightly drawn in its moderation. Quoting Diderot, he says that one must be prudent, but "with a great disdain for prudence." Thus, his "love" for democracy is, like Tocqueville's, quite mod-

[22] "El poeta en su tierra," interview with Braulio Peralta, in *OC* vol. 15, p. 389.

erate: the affection of a skeptic. This is why he viewed the arrival of democracy to Mexico with a mixture of pleasure and concern.

> The creation of a healthy democracy demands the recognition of the Other and of Others. The response to the questions many of us have asked regarding the situation in Mexico after July sixth concerns first and foremost the leaders of political parties. A policy of vengeance or the imposition of reforms that would find repudiation among broad sectors of public opinion [...] would lead us to what we fear most: disputes, agitations, disorder and, in the end, instability, that mother of two twins, anarchy and force. [...] Impunity is just as bad as intolerance. What we need in order to ensure our future is moderation, that is to say, *prudence,* the highest of political virtues according to the ancient philosophers. Mexico has always lived between two extremes: dictatorship and anarchy, right and left, clericalism and Jacobinism. We have almost always lacked a center, and that is why our history has been a long failure. Prudence, the natural enemy of extremes, is a bridge of peaceful transit from authoritarianism to democracy.

I said before that politics was not one of Paz's passions. That isn't true. Politics was the permanent shadow cast by his two great passions: liberty and its pinprick, criticism. That is why Octavio Paz was so passionate about politics, no matter how accursed they are.

Yesterday is a question. What has already happened is as uncertain as what has not yet taken place. Memory, Paz says, is a garden of doubts, a path of echoes, a muddy mirror. Remembrance implies attending to murmurs, shadows of thought, rumors, fantasies, and obliterations.

> Time never stops flowing,
>   time
> never stops creating,
>   time never stops
> erasing its creations,
>   the spring
> of visions never stops.[23]

In the basket of the past, Octavio Paz seeks out the fig tree of his childhood, the Constitution of his country, the meaning of art, the passage of civilizations, the childhood of his beloved, the variations of poetry. The search for himself and others as an expedition through time. Memory is the lantern that allows us to trace the tradition of criticism or trap the family scorpions. I write here memory, not History, because in Paz memory seems to unfold into two rival formulas. The memory is the past vivified in images; History is a concluded past. Two forms of remembrance, memory and history, do battle: poetics against the politics of the past. Whereas History condemns us, memory can save us.

All of Paz's essays are soaked in memory. Each one contains some reflection about the origin and transformation of what can be observed: a painting, a poem, an empire. Even more so than in his essays, the image of the de-

---

[23] "Facing Time," *The Collected Poems of Octavio Paz*, trans. Eliot Weinberger, p. 394.

mon of history is forcefully drawn in his poetry, above all in that of his maturity. To start with, his distancing from Joyce: history is not a nightmare.[24] It isn't that he fails to find consolation in the act of awakening. We cannot peel ourselves away from history by pinching our arms, we exist within it and thanks to it. But history can be, if not a macabre nightmare, an iron gallows. This is what it becomes when the course of time is detained within the wells of ideology. This is why Paz writes in "Although it is night": "Stalin had no soul: he had history." Those who believe they have deciphered the secrets of the past will soon adhere to the cause of tyranny. History, he says a few lines later in the same poem, is "discourse on a frozen blade."

His great friend, the English poet Charles Tomlinson, wrote a poem that adopts the same image: Stalin and his assassins, brandishing the ice pick of history. This poem bears, in fact, an epigraph by Paz and was translated by the Mexican poet, who commented on it in a brief essay.[25]

> I strike. I am the future and my blow
> Will have it now. If lightning froze
> It would hover as here, the room
> Riding in the crest of the moment's wave,
> In the deed's time, the deed's transfiguration

[24] He said this upon receiving the Tocqueville Prize in 1989. Forty years earlier, in *The Labyrinth of Solitude*, he said exactly the opposite: "History has the atrocious reality of a nightmare; the grandeur of man consists of making beautiful, lasting works out of the actual substance of that nightmare. Or to put it another way, transfiguring the nightmare as vision; freeing ourselves, albeit for an instant, from shapeless reality via creation," (p. 114).

[25] "The assassin and eternity," in *OC* vol. 9, p. 104.

And as if that wave would never again recede.

I am the future; my dagger embeds future in the world. As far as the tyrant is concerned, history becomes a perfect substitute for a conscience. There is where all theories that sustain historic inevitability unfold, in the elimination of individual responsibility. It is the same intellectual equation described by Isaiah Berlin: if history has been transformed into logic, the only sensible thing to do is to adhere to victorious reason. Whoever takes that side is wise; those who position themselves at the forefront are retrogrades who must be eliminated. That is why the historian of ideas said that once we have adopted the mechanics of historic necessity, moral judgment becomes absurd. Attila, Robespierre, Hitler, Stalin are earthquakes: natural forces that inevitably burst into history. Censuring their crimes is tantamount to admonishing lettuce.[26]

This mode of capturing the past is the "deathtrap into which the fanatic who believes he possesses the secret of history invariably falls." Crime thus takes on a philosophical dignity: the extermination of a category of men is considered to be a duty among those who have learned the lessons of time. The past becomes an extermination manual, a precedent for concentration camps. Popper called all of this historicism: the libretto of history, once revealed, turns many men into waste.

Paz himself was inebriated by the liquor of history:

Good, we wanted good:

---

[26] Isaiah Berlin, "Historical inevitability," in *Four Essays on Liberty* (Oxford: Oxford University Press, 1990).

to set the world right.
We didn't lack integrity:
we lacked humility.
What we wanted was not innocently wanted.
Precepts and concepts,
the arrogance of theologians,
to beat with a cross,
to institute with blood,
to build the house with bricks of crime,
to declare obligatory communion.
Some
became secretaries to the secretary
to the General Secretary of the Inferno.
Rage
became philosophy,
its drivel has covered the planet.
Reason came down to earth,
took the form of a gallows
--and is worshipped by millions.[27]

One might say that, together with a concern for language, Paz's poetry is marked by a concern for history. His restlessness was always present, but it intensified as the poet matured. History and with it, politics, penetrate the poetry of a man of the city, a writer who always wanted to converse with his peers: "I have written about history and history in our century takes the shape of politics. The 'destiny' of the ancients wears the mask of politics in the

[27] *The Collected Poems of Octavio Paz*, trans. Eliot Weinberger, "San Ildefonso nocturne," pp. 419-420.

20th century."[28] And the story of 20th-century politics is one of failure: Hitler, Stalin, Franco; two world wars, totalitarianism, empires, terrorism, bombs, dictatorships, genocides. In the retelling, history is portrayed as nonsense, madness, emptiness: "Being time is a conviction. Our sentence is history."

> Everything we think of is undone,
> in the Fields utopia is incarnate,
> history is a spiral with no outcome.

And yet, in the history that is dementia, crime, and absurdity there is also hope. Once more, opposites embrace. Thus history no longer appears as an alibi, but as enlightenment. Beyond history, there is memory. If the politics of history intends to throw the past into the realm of Nature, the poetics of memory bathes the past in the waters of the imagination. There, the hidden relationships between things are revealed. The historian, Paz says, must have a bit of the scientist and a great deal of the poet. The man of science hunts down laws, rules that explain reiteration. The poet, on the other hand, turns to the unique, the unrepeatable. That is why the historian's task lies between one world and the next. He studies the unrepeatable, seeking out the shroud that envelops it.

The historian does not discover, and he does not invent: he remakes the past. Diving into the past is another way to perform criticism. This isn't about approaching our history in order to comprehend our selves, but rather

---

28 "To converse is human," interview with Enrico Mario Santí, in *OC* vol. 15, p. 545.

about approaching the past in order to free our selves. The criticism of history is where the possibilities of liberty unfold. That was Paz's task when he reconstructed the past of Mexico, that suffocating land that fascinated him always. Looking behind the facts, behind the walls, behind gestures and their masks. The poet seeks the symbols through which time and space flirt with us. "The history of Mexico," he writes in his essay about Sor Juana, "is a history in the likeness and image of its geography: abrupt, anfractuous. Each historical period is like a butte surrounded by high mountains, separated from all the rest by precipices and cliffs."[29] From one century to another, the abyss; a crag between one decade and the next. The Conquest is determined to bury the pre-Colombian world. Independence and, above all, the triumphant liberal project intend to break away from the Catholic universe of New Spain. Two frustrated negations. Despite the burning of idols and destruction of codices, the Indian world survived. Despite the new rules and constitutions, the world of New Spain survived. Fruitless denials.

The universe is a trunk full of symbols that the imagination must exhume. When in *The Labyrinth of Solitude* Paz attempts to reconstruct the meaning of the Conquest, he closes his eyes and he imagines. He does not recur, as disciplined historians do, to the dust of documents or the dry ink of letters. Breaking all the rules of historiography, the poet positions himself in the universe of Moctezuma and imagines his drama.

---

[29] Octavio Paz, *Sor Juana Inés de la Cruz or The traps of faith* (Mexico: Fondo de Cultura Económica, 1982), p. 24.

> Why does Moctezuma give in? Why does he feel strangely fascinated by the Spaniards and experience before them a vertigo that we can call, without fear of exaggeration, sacred –the lucid vertigo of a suicidal man on the brink of the abyss? The gods have abandoned him. The great betrayal with which the history of Mexico begins is neither that of the Tlaxcaltecans, nor that of Moctezuma and his group, but rather of the gods. No other people have felt so totally helpless as the Aztec nation did before the warnings, prophecies, and signs that announced its fall.[30]

This paragraph would fill academic historians with indignation. There is no glimmer of proof or document to sustain Paz's statements. Vertigo of suicide? Betrayal of the gods? The poet does not intend to grasp a historic reality, he wants to evoke its image. In order to understand the meaning of that historic image, we must turn to Paz's writings about poetry. In the first place, the historic silhouettes that Paz outlines express *his* experience of history: they are authentic. To put it in two different phrases from the same poem, the *past clarified* is *time within*.[31] Second, these images find a logic of their own: they hold the truth of their own existence. The image "is worthwhile only within its own universe." Finally, the image also speaks of the world and has an objective foundation. The poetic image of history is a legitimate, powerful way to capture reality. It is not the detailed narration of events, scenarios, and outcomes, it is the instantaneous and total presence of time passed. Compressed moments. Nor

[30] *The Labyrinth of Solitude*, in *OC* vol. 8, p. 107.

[31] As Paz relates in his letters to Gimferrer, the first title of *Past Clarified* was, precisely, *Time Within*.

is the image lost in explanations. The reconstruction of history is never traced from the past. It is something altogether different: its recreation.

Poetry turns past into present. This is one of its functions as collective memory. "Poetry exorcizes the past; thus the present becomes inhabitable." When history is illuminated by poetry, all times are in this now. "The poem is the house of presence. Woven from words made of air, the poem is infinitely fragile and yet, infinitely resistant. It is a perpetual challenge to the gravity of history."[32] Against leaden history, the air of memory.

On December 17, 1997, Octavio Paz appeared for the last time in public. Using a wheelchair, he entered the patio of the old Alvarado House to find the Republic of Mexico paying tribute to him. He was surrounded by the president and his ministers, by entrepreneurs and men of letters. Pained by each breath of air he took, Paz recalled his grandfather and Díaz Mirón. At one moment, he raised his head and looked up into the sky of Coyoacán. Bewitching his audience, the poet spoke of his friends, his childhood, his wife; of his desire when he was a boy to be the trumpet, not the sword; of the generosity and mystery of words, the sun and clouds of Mexico, the lightness and darkness of his fatherland, that blend of bright and shadows that always intrigued him. He concluded with a request: "May we be worthy of the clouds and sun of the Valley of Mexico." Gabriel Zaid would later recall that morning: "It was a gray day, but he began to talk about

[32] *OC* vol. 1, p. 27.

the sun, about thankfulness and grace. The most moving of all was that the sun, as if called upon to take part in the conversation, appeared." This is true. I was there.

Up until his last breath, Paz reeled off the syllables of Mexico, trying to decipher the mystery of its sound, seeking out its form, its soul. Ever since *The Labyrinth of Solitude* was published, this fatherland of "Castille with Aztec stripes" was Paz's *idée fixe*. Nothing Mexican was alien to him. The essayist wrote about the skirt of Coatlicue and the carols of Sor Juana, about sapodilla, tortilla, and mole sauce; he meditated on portraits by Hermenegildo Bustos, landscapes by Velazco, and Tamayo's incandescent fruit. Jaguars, eagles, Virgins, skeletons. Paz caressed the shape of Mexico, traveling across its history, interrogating its geography, unraveling the skein of its public life. Hundreds, thousands of pages that compose, as he would say, a diary in search of his country and himself: the quest for a place, the quest for himself. A pilgrim in his own homeland.[33] Mexico was for him a passion that was not always joyful. Above all it was a responsibility: to interpret Mexican existence was to make its history. Zaid well understood this commitment as he watched him submit to a destiny that "he assumes as his duty: history asking to be made":

> It is not the same to write in a country that takes itself for granted, in a culture that is inhabitable beyond the slightest doubt, as part of a lifelong project that can be accommodated within established social niches that consider creation to be part of a

[33] "Entrada retrospectiva," prologue to *OC* vol. 8: *El peregrino en su patria. Historia y política en México*, p. 16.

> specialized career; as to write while feeling the urgent need to create or recreate everything: language, the culture of life, the insertion into nation-building itself, all of this can become *oeuvre* in the broadest creative sense.[34]

Indeed, Paz's task was Promethean: to embrace all spaces of a culture in order to make it inhabitable, to activate it as conversant with world culture. The Mexico question would never abandon Paz. Halfway through the century, in *The Labyrinth of Solitude*, that book that was interpreted as "an elegant insult," portrays the Mexican as a being who disguises himself: "a face, a mask and a smile, a mask." He didn't *define* the Mexican, he excavated his hieroglyph. Twenty years later he would write in *Postdata* that to be Mexican was not an essence, but a history. In any case, Mexico and its population would continue to be a central question. Mexico, its history, its geography, its art: nouns that find both verb and predicate in Octavio Paz's essay.

This is, perhaps, the most badly bruised fig in Paz's basket. Despite all of his warnings about the flow of history and its surprises, despite his certainty regarding the universal delta of our province ("we are, for the first time in our history, contemporaries of all men"); despite his early and energetic opposition to nationalism gone astray, he couldn't stop toying with the artifices of identity. With the imaginary anatomy of nationhood. Nowhere can the curve of this identitary hook be observed with greater clarity than in the contrast Paz constantly makes between

[34] Gabriel Zaid, "Octavio Paz y la emancipación cultural," in *Ensayos sobre poesía, Obras 2* (Mexico: El Colegio Nacional, 1993).

Mexico and the United States. Antagonistic physical entities, biological species that cannot be coupled, Mexico and the United States are not intertwined: they are confronted in his essays.

> They are credulous, we are believers; they love fairy tales and detective stories, we love myths and legends. Mexicans lie out of fantasy, despair, or to overcome their sordid lives; they do not lie, but they substitute the actual truth, which is always disagreeable, with a social truth. We get drunk to confess; they do so to forget. They are optimists, we are nihilists –except that our nihilism is not an intellectual, but rather an instinctive reaction: it is, therefore, irrefutable. Mexicans are mistrustful; they are open. We are sad and sarcastic; they are happy and humorous. Americans want to comprehend, we want to contemplate...[35]

And later on: "The solitude of the Mexican is one of stagnant waters, that of the North American is the mirror." Therefore, when Mexicans cross the border, they are like drops of water in a well of oil. Even in the late 1970s, Paz insisted on the insurmountable differences between the two countries. Two different versions of the Western world. When he examined the paths taken by these neighbors throughout the centuries, he approached an ice-cold reading of history. The founding of a society appears to seal its fate. They are the sons of Reform, we are the descendents of Counter-Reform. That is why he states, almost with pride, that Mexicans who emigrate to the Unit-

---

[35] This is the chapter on "El Pachuco y otros extremos," from *El laberinto de la soledad*, in *OC* vol. 8, p. 57.

ed States are incapable of adapting to American society: they have retained their identity. And he makes, thus, a frankly conservative defense of "resistance" to the outside: "our country survives thanks to its traditionalism."[36] Custom as survival.

In these lines, captivated by the matron of identity, the poet turned a deaf ear to the reasoning of Jorge Cuesta, whom he so greatly admired. Paz met him in San Ildefonso in 1935. The young man approached the critic and soon embarked on a conversation that would be continued at a German restaurant in downtown Mexico City. "We talked about Lawrence and Huxley, that is to say, about passion and reason; about Gide and Malraux, that is to say, about curiosity and action."[37] This conversation between poets would never end.

Jorge Cuesta's portraits form part of a mysterious gallery. Luis Cardoza y Aragón draws him as an ugly man who was besieged by women. A Picasso portrait of sorts, with one eye higher than the other. A jovial shark. A watchmaker who took apart the pieces of an argument in order to put them back together again in such a way that his logic would always triumph. At one point, Xavier Villaurrutia felt compelled to provide his testimony that this man existed only because there were those who doubted it. He was believed to be a tapestry of myths, and yet he was made of flesh and blood. He was a man who devoured all: philosophy, aesthetics, science, poetry. Everything attracted him with the same force, anything enabled him

---

[36] "El espejo indiscreto," in *OC* vol. 8, p. 434.

[37] "Contemporáneos," in *OC* vol. 4, p. 72.

to set in motion the dexterity of his wit. Salvador Novo described him as a clever and unbalanced boy. What his hands touched, Ermilio Abreu Gómez would say, turned to ashes, to dust. By all accounts, he was highly intelligent, tall, and thin. Elías Nandino emphasized his long, bony hands, his angelical and satanic aura in which intelligence and intuition come together: magic and microscope. His untamed character was also noted. Under the wooden angelic image was hidden a blasphemous tempest, a lethal deposit of irony. A phantom, a man alienated from his body. When he spoke, people listened not knowing where his words came from; it seemed as if they surged from the phantoms of the air. And Octavio Paz rendered his eyes of perpetual amazement, his elegance, his strange Afro-British physiognomy. A man who did not serve himself intelligence but rather, served intelligence; a man possessed by the fearsome god of Reason, a man who lacked common sense, that dose of intuition, or perhaps irrationality, that we need to live.

But as I was saying, Paz turned a deaf ear to Cuesta, who insisted that Mexico needed to row *against* its past and staunchly combat the frauds of nationalists or identitarians who were, in this case, one and the same. Identity, no matter what its packaging, locks us up in a cage. That was the problem: Paz never stopped asking himself which body we inhabit. One might talk about identity from the discourse of race, the divan of psychoanalysis, or the image of poetic myth. In the end, its trophy catch is only a fishnet that both falsifies and hinders.

THAT AFTERNOON ON DECEMBER 17, ONCE THE POLITICIANS and magnates had left the house in Coyoacán where Octavio Paz resided, the poet lingered for a while with his wife and a few close friends. Christopher Domínguez describes the scene. Despite the pain of his illness, the same lucidity and wit as always would sudenly appear. Someone informed him that his friend Claude Roy had died, and he shed a few tears.

> Then he decided to talk about death. About his own death. "When I found out how gravely ill I was," he said, "I realized that I could not take the sublime road of Christianity. I do not believe in transcendence. The idea of extinction has set me at ease. I shall become this glass of water I am drinking. I shall become matter."[38]

---

[38] "The Death of Octavio Paz," in *La sabiduría sin promesa. Vidas y letras del siglo XX* (Mexico: Joaquín Mortiz, 2001), p. 333.